HEALING
THROUGH

and
"FROM SARITA'S PEN"

HEALING THROUGH

and

"FROM SARITA'S PEN"

Inspiring and Motivating Through My Pain

SARITA PRICE

authorHOUSE®

AuthorHouse™ LLC
1663 Liberty Drive
Bloomington, IN 47403
www.authorhouse.com
Phone: 1-800-839-8640

Editor, Dr. Denise Lofton

Published by AuthorHouse   01/21/2014

ISBN: 978-1-4918-3093-2 (sc)
ISBN: 978-1-4918-3092-5 (hc)
ISBN: 978-1-4918-3131-1 (e)

Library of Congress Control Number: 2013919674

TABLE OF CONTENTS

DEDICATION

I dedicate this work to my late father, Lee Arthur Robertson, (December 1925-May 1989), who laid the foundation of *perseverance* for me. He was my motivation and inspiration. It was through him that I learned how to work hard and push through obstacles. Your love still guides me. I miss you deeply Daddy.

I dedicate this work to every man and woman who help transform lives while pushing through the ugliness of divorce and dealing with his or her own pain. You moved forward to be all God called you to be.

ACKNOWLEDGEMENTS

To my Jehovah God, the eternal self-existing one who keeps his covenant promises to his covenant people. You are my ALL and the center of my joy. I am who I am because of you, THE GREAT I AM

To The First Lady of The New Olivet Baptist Church, Sheila Whalum, it is because of your beauty, grace and words of encouragement that I am a self-assured woman. You were the angel God sent to help pull me out of the valley of low self-esteem. You are so important to me, and I love you.

To Qualice Seymour, thank you my sister in the ministry for encouraging me to continue writing even when I had no desire to write a book. You once told me that I would know when it was time to publish the book. Love you Lady.

To my new found friend, Vikki Kennedy Johnson, no words can express how you have TRULY blessed me and how your words of wisdom have helped transform my life. Because you are authentic and so loving, I am inspired to continue to truly give back and help other women through the restoration process. I love you. Yes, we are sisters.

To my former supervisor Keith Traster, you truly don't know how your words of encouragement in the work place helped to change my life. You were always there pushing me through graduate school and providing me with honest feedback on my papers. But what I remember most was how you would open up your office to me when I was going through my divorce, and allow me to cry in private. You never said a word; you just gave me a box of tissue and let me have my moment. Thank you (smile)

To my former co-worker Derestine Young, thank you for being a true prayer warrior who interceded for me, encouraged me, and spoke words of prophecy over my life. And yes, they are manifesting.

To my little mini me Semira Price, I love you. You are the main reason I keep going. You are growing up to be such an anointed and beautiful young lady. I know God has amazing blessings ahead just for you. Love you Pooh

To my family, friends, teachers, and mentors, thank you so much for your love and support. You were there when *From Sarita's Pen* was just an idea. You shared with me how the inspirations blessed you. Little did you know your words of encouragement blessed me to move forward, and to publish this book.

INTRODUCTION

God has truly blessed me to go into and excel in areas I could never have imagined. Writing frightened me in high school and yes, even in college. But it just shows, when you allow God in your life, he will anoint you to do things you thought impossible. God does not call the qualified, he qualifies the called. Selah (Stop and think about it).

Healing Through and From Sarita's Pen is unique because the inspirational and motivational quotes and prayers were designed to be a blessing to others even while I was going through hurt, pain and the disappointment of divorce. As a preacher, a teacher, and a leader in my church, and I was going through this unthinkable situation. But then, God gave me Jeremiah 29:11 (NLT); "For I know the plans I have for you, says the Lord. They are plans for good and not for disaster, to give you a future and a hope." It was then that I changed my perspective of why he wanted me to write. The writing was not for me, it was to help others. Yet in the process of writing, I was being healed. All the trials and tribulations I was going through became less and less traumatic. While I was focusing on helping others, God handled my issues. Obedience is better than sacrifice. God told me he had a new beginning waiting for me, but I must let go of the past. He told me to not let the enemy keep me depressed and discouraged. He would not let one door close without opening another one for me. When the devil reminds me of my past, remind him of his future. I wrote almost daily, contributing to the healing of others, and *being* healed at the same time.

After five years of taking theology classes, teaching, and preaching, it was in 2008 that I started to truly understand and apply Hebrews 4:2 that states to mix the word of God with faith in order to profit from the word of God. It was during this time as well that I started shifting from 'religion to relationship' with God. *From Sarita's Pen* is inspiration given to me through the word of God, with boldness and authenticity to help others deal with everyday life. God will give you the desires of your heart, 'if' you will submit to Him. *From Sarita's Pen* is the result of me finally submitting to God's will and trusting Him all the way. But most importantly, *From Sarita's Pen* is me showing my love for God and His people.

Peace: Internal Peace

Only God Can Give

DON'T HATE ON MY PEACE

Don't become annoyed, envious or jealous of others who have inner peace just because you don't possess what you desire. Peace comes from within. Clear away the trash first, and maybe peace will find a way in.—*From Sarita's Pen*

SCRIPTURE . . . .

Titus 3:3 (KJV)

For we ourselves also were sometimes foolish, disobedient, deceived, serving divers lusts and pleasures, living in malice and envy, hateful, and hating one another.

James 3:16 (KJV)

For where envying and strife is, there is confusion and every evil work.

Colossians 3:15(NLT)

And let the peace that comes from Christ rule in your hearts. For as members of one body you are called to live in peace. And always be thankful

PRAYER

God, I pray that you will continue to give me a humble spirit. I pray and proclaim that I will continue to move forward in what you will have me to do and not be distracted by the enemy and his workers. You stated in your word that you would make my enemies my foot stool and protect me from their attacks. I believe that right now. God, I know that the road would not be easy and there would be roadblocks. But God, you stated in Psalm 27:2 (NLT) that when evil people come to devour me, when my enemies and foes attack me, they will stumble and fall. I believe that and I am standing on your word. God, I am also believing and proclaiming Psalm 54:5 that the evil plans of my enemies be turned against them. God do as you promised and put an end to them. God, I pray for our children. I pray a covering over them. I pray that the school will continue to be an institution for learning and not a war zone. I speak blessings and a covering for the elected officials in the city who are working for you. Give them strength to endure. For in their well doing, they shall be blessed. I speak peace in the areas of confusion. I pray that you will infuse them with power to take charge of the situation in your name. There is no room for fear and doubt. Every word that has been spoken, God, I proclaim it, pronounce it, and decree it. Victory is ours and the enemy and his workers are already defeated. It is so!!! Amen. ***Flowing From Sarita's Heart & Pen***

WHAT R U KNOWN FOR: A TITLE ONLY OR A TESTIMONY?

INSPIRED THOUGHTS . . . .

Titles are a good thing and according to the world standards, it can open or even shut doors for you. But the question you may want to ask yourself is what will people say about you when you are gone from this earth. Will they know you by a title only or the works you have done? One does not necessarily correlates with the other. Be known for your good works, because during the process, you will have trials and test. Test brings about testimonies and your testimonies could be life changing blessings for others.—*From Sarita's Pen*

SCRIPTURE

Psalm 18:27 (21st Century KJV)

For Thou wilt save the afflicted people, but wilt bring down haughty looks.

Psalm 131:1 *(KJV)*

Lord, my heart is not haughty, nor mine eyes lofty: neither do I exercise myself in great matters, or in things too high for me.

John 14:12 (NLT)

"I tell you the truth, anyone who believes in me will do the same works I have done, and even greater works, because I am going to be with the Father

PRAYER:

God, I thank you for another day and another word that keeps me going higher and higher. God I pray not to be selfish with the blessings that you have given me. God I will share my testimonies of your goodness. I am your child. Because I am your child, I am special, and have greater works to do. God, I am so glad that you do not call the qualified, but qualify the called. God, I have experienced the power that you have given, but it is up to your people to tap into it. I pray this pray with humility. Amen!!! ***Flowing From Sarita's Heart/Pen***

YOU CAN'T MOVE
FORWARD UNTIL _____

You can't move into what God has for you because 1) You have a negative attitude 2) You don't know "who you are" 3) You don't forgive and 4)You don't realize that you are A Gift.—*From Sarita's Pen*

SCRIPTURE

Philippians 3:14 (KJV)

I press toward the mark for the prize of the high calling of God in Christ Jesus.

Prayer

Well God. Once again you have done exceedingly above what I could have imagined! Your mercy and grace cannot be measured. Thank you for giving, giving, giving and giving. You blessed me even in my mess. Thank you for the correction in love. God, I thank You for every person reading this prayer and pray that they spread what has been given to them. I pray they spread the blessings. I pray that selfishness will diminish more and more each day. God you said in Genesis that you made us in your image. God, I pray that I start reflecting this more daily. I pray daily to see through your eyes. I pray to love others with your love, and look beyond their faults and see their needs. I proclaim decree and call it in existence LORD that higher grounds are mine. But God, I am aware that with higher levels come bigger devils. God, I am not worried, because nothing will happen that you and I can't handle. IT IS SO! Amen. ***Flowing From Sarita's Heart & Pen.***

"Re"unite with The Lover of Your Soul

The year 2010 was a year of new beginnings and the year of "Re—(afresh; anew). If you have a list of relationships you are seeking to re-establish, make sure God is at the top of that list. Reuniting with Him first could make the list shorter and the process easier. There may be some relationships that are not meant to be re-established. God is your guide and your ultimate counselor.—*From Sarita's Pen*

Scripture

1 John 4:16 (KJV)

And we have known and believed the love that God hath to us. God is love; and he that dwelleth in love dwelleth in God, and God in him.

Prayer

God, I thank you for your unconditional love. I pray that I as well as others follow in your footsteps. Loving people with unconditional love can be very difficult, but with you God, all things are possible. Thank you once again for a day that was not promised. You are always on time and faithful. Create in me a clean heart and renew in me a right spirit. Remove any anger, malice, and hate toward others from my heart. You, O God are the final judge. I pray for a closer relationship with you and with clarity. I also pray the readers of this prayer will do the same. You are the author and finisher of our fate. Some may have been hurt or disappointed by someone from their past. But God, you are a healer and the God of second chances. With every painful situation comes a lesson and forgiveness should always be present. You are the lover of my soul and in you, I will always trust. Amen!!! ***Flowing From Sarita's Heart & Pen.***

LET IT GO AND FLOW

In this journey, death is a part of life. Not just physical death, but in the spiritual realm also. Some 'things' must die in order for you to receive new. Let things go that really do not matter so God can give you *The New*. Go with the flow of God and not against his movement. 'Be' who you are called to be. It's not always about the doing, but about just 'being'. God wants you to live a good life of health and wellness. Stand and live on God's spoken word. Think on the positive things in life because consistently thinking on the negative will go against all things that God has. Negative thinking will not only upset your spirit, but it will eventually distress your health. Live and not die. I choose life. Will you?— **From Sarita's Pen**

SCRIPTURE

Philippians 4:8 (NLT)

And now, dear brothers and sisters, one final thing. Fix your thoughts on what is true, and honorable, and right, and pure, and lovely, and admirable. Think about things that are excellent and worthy of praise.

PRAYER

God today I petition Your throne of grace for those who are hurting and who are at the end of their rope. I speak a word of patience to those who want to take matters into their own hands. You are the all mighty God and You don't need our help. God, I pray that You will move on our behalf and transform the strife

Sarita Price

into serenity. God, cast down every stronghold in our lives and let us release all to You so that You can handle the situation. Two wrongs never make a right. Mature us in You God as hearts and minds are transformed. You state in Romans 12:19 (NLT) "Dearly beloved, avenge not yourselves, but rather give place unto wrath: for it is written, Vengeance is mine; I will repay, saith the Lord". God, I have learned that You can handle my enemies a great deal better than me. When I let You have the situation, I am blessed and You place me at a higher level. God give our people the strength to endure and focus on the things that really matter while You handle the situation. For those who refuse to listen to You, forgive them and give them the strength to endure what will come to pass due to disobedience. We all must answer for our transgressions. But, God, I am believing You will soften hearts and in the end, You will get the glory. IT IS SO! Amen. **From Sarita' Heart & Pen.**

GETTING A BALANCE AND DOING THE RIGHT THINGS

Sometimes we as Christians become so overwhelm with 'doing church work' that we become unbalanced in our day to day lives. We neglect our homes, families, and yes, even our jobs. But one thing we must remember is that we can't let our 'do' overtake our 'who'. Who we are in Christ should determine what we do for His Kingdom. You must have balance in your life and God wants that also. Love, laugh and just live. You can serve God in many areas of your life. Loving and spending time with family, friends, and people in general is a way of serving Him. Greater works we must do, but even Jesus took time to rest.—**From Sarita's Pen**

SCRIPTURE

Matthew 11:28 (NLT)

Then Jesus said, "Come to me, all of you who are weary and carry heavy burdens, and I will give you rest.

2 Samuel 22:33 (KJV)

God is my strength and power: and he maketh my way perfect.

PRAYER

God, I thank You for restoring my peace. God, I come to You this afternoon with an attitude of gratitude. Thank You for the power of prayer and worship. God, I come interceding for my sisters and brothers who have reached out to me. God, I know and claim right now that You will work everything out for their good. It may not be according to their wishes, BUT You God know best. God, I claim that many will take back what the devil has taken from them. Satan is and has been very busy these last few months as I have witnessed the havoc he has caused in others' lives and from personal experience. But today, I put him on notice that he gets nothing, and You God receive all the glory. What he tried to destroy did not come to pass but the joy of God prevailed. I pray death unto all that Satan is planning right now against Your children. He will not win because victory is already ours. God, I pray that Your people will change their thought process, and focus on the good things in life and not always the bad. We all have something to be thankful for. God, I bless You right now. I look forward to living life well in Christ. I pray the same for my sisters and brothers in Christ. God, You are my joy. You make me happy. Amen! **Flowing from Sarita's Heart & Pen**

It's Hard Out Here
For A Christian

This is a season of transformation and many are experiencing broken and battered faith. But I tell you do not give up. Your destination has not changed. God will give you the strength and ability to manage the detours. Keep forgiveness and humility in your heart and prepare for the promise.—**From Sarita's Pen**

SCRIPTURE

Revelation 14:12 (NLT)

This means that God's holy people must endure persecution patiently, obeying his commands and maintaining their faith in Jesus.

Galatians 6:9 (NLT)

So let's not get tired of doing what is good. At just the right time we will reap a harvest of blessing if we don't give up.

PRAYER

God, I thank You today for clarity, and for eye opening experiences. God, I thank You today for strength not just for me, but for my sisters and brothers who are broken. God, I intercede for them and pray their strength. It's hard for Christians especially in times like these. But You, O God, are still in charge and in the blessing business. You tell us to cast our cares on You.

Many are experiencing brokenness, but God, I am here to let all know there is strength in being broken. Brokenness allows for humility and peace to manifest. God, from experience, I have learned that when peace is present, this is the time You, God, will come in and work on Your children. You infuse us with Your spirit resulting in power to move forward in boldness not caring what anyone may think or say. God, I pray that my sisters and brothers learn to how to inject Your word in their everyday lives. Let them know that You can be a Christian and still be successful in business, school, and all areas of life. True advancement or promotion does not come from man, but from You God (Psalm 75:6-7). You have our destiny in Your hands and we can make it if we just keep the faith. God, You continue to tell us in Your word that the war has already been won many years ago on the cross. It is up to us not to get caught up in the ways of darkness which may be camouflaged in many behaviors. Staying close to You God is the answer to handling the enemy's tricks. You will show favor and provide protection. Thank You!!!!!! Amen. **Flowing From Sarita's Heart & Pen.**

Be Patient: Your Time Is Coming !!!

Many times in life, we feel that we should always be on the 'mountain top'. We don't want to experience the 'valley' moments. But without the valley moments, we can't grow. Preparation is necessary. Moses spent 40 years in preparation. Paul spent a great deal of his life working toward the wrong purpose until a dramatic event changed his life. Jacob spent 20 years working for Laban. The day to day working life molds us and makes us into what God desires. God may still be preparing you for something far greater. Stay faithful.—*From Sarita's Pen*

Scripture

Psalm 37:34 (NKJV)

Wait on the LORD and keep His way, and He shall exalt thee to inherit the land; when the wicked are cut off, thou shalt see it.

Prayer

Thank You for this day that was not promised to me. I thank You for a new day and a new beginning. Lord, I thank You for a new mindset. It's not about me, but about You and ministering to people. I thank You for Your angels on earth You send to minister to me. Lord there is none like You and no one can love me like You. I thank You for the valley experiences that make me a stronger and better person. God, I see daily that the enemy is 'more' real and focused on doing his job, BUT You always flip the script on him and turn it around in my favor. God, I pray for those no one else is praying for. I pray for my brothers and sisters who are hurt, angry, bitter, lost, confused and battling with the flesh. I speak peace into their lives and I pray that they will return to You. Their lives will never ever be the same. I pray that all will resist Satan and call on Your name. At the name of Jesus, demons will flee. God, You will and have equipped each of us to fight the enemy and win. We must yield and stay close to You. God, I thank You for clarity and the boldness to face my enemies. God, I am tired of the enemy causing confusion and chaos in my life and the lives of Your people. God, I pray that each of us will declare war on the enemy and take back what he has taken. The battle starts in the mind and each of us must win that war. God, I pray that each of us will stop entertaining mess and the little demons that the enemy can place before us, even if they look harmless. God, I speak a new life and cast down every form of witchcraft that the enemy tries to create. He may be strong, but You are the ALMIGHTY GOD. So Satan, You are being put on notice. You and Your works will be destroyed. We, as God's children, are tired and we are about to shake the foundations of hell with the power that our Father has given us. We will fast and pray prayers that we have never prayed before. We will stand bold in Christ, from our house to the White House. We will rise up and educate the future generations of saints to fight You Satan, and Your kingdom. No longer will we stand for mediocrity. EXCELLENCE in Christ is the *new*. I declare it; decree and it ALL shall come to pass. Amen, Amen, and Amen!!! ***Strongly Flowing From Sarita's Heart & Pen***

RELATIONSHIPS: GOD WANTS TO BE FIRST IN YOUR LIFE . . . . NOT 31ST !!!

INSPIRED THOUGHTS . . .

Many times we cause our own problems by putting things and people before we do God. God is a jealous God, and he will not continue to tolerate disobedience. Just think of it this way, as a parent, would you continue to let your children disrespect and slap you in the face especially if you have taken care of and love them? If you are God's child, why do you think He will continue to let you do the same to him? *Selah* (stop and think about it)— ***From Sarita's Pen***

SCRIPTURE

Exodus 34:14 (KVJ)

For thou shalt worship no other god: for the LORD, whose name is Jealous, is a jealous God:

PRAYER

Today God, I come thanking You for Your divine blessings and favor on my life. I thank You most of all for the Holy Spirit that keeps me aware and alert. God, today I pray for relationships. I pray especially for those who need to seek and make You first in their lives. God, I pray that each of us will spend more time with You not just at church, but in a more intimate setting daily. You, God are the source of our being, and You have the authority and power to change all our lives so that we CAN live in peace, power, protection and prosperity. Luke 12:21 (NLT) tells us that only a fool would store up earthly wealth but not have a rich relationship with You. Also, 2 John 1:9 (NLT) further tells us that anyone who wanders away from Your teaching has no relationship with You. But anyone who remains in the teaching of Christ has a relationship with both the Father and the Son. God, I pray that each of us will set our priorities straight and spend more time with You. The outcome is awesome and our lives will never ever be the same. I'm just speaking from experience, and watching You work. Amen. ***Flowing From Sarita's Pen***

HEALING: R U STILL HURTING?
PLEASE LET HIM HAVE IT!

INSPIRED THOUGHTS . . .

God has a new beginning waiting for you, but you must let go of the past. Don't let the enemy keep you where you are. God will not allow one door to close without opening another one for you. When the devil reminds you of your past, you remind him of his future—**From Sarita's Pen**

SCRIPTURE

Psalm 55:22 (NLT)

Give your burdens to the Lord, and he will take care of you. He will not permit the godly to slip and fall

Psalm 138:7 (NLT)

Though I am surrounded by troubles, you will protect me from the anger of my enemies. You reach out your hand, and the power of your right hand saves me.

John 14:18 (NLT)

No, I will not abandon you as orphans—I will come to you.

PRAYER

God, I come to You today with a troubled spirit praying for my sister(s) and brother(s) who are holding on to past hurt and pain.

God, I pray they will give their hurt to You. They have given them to You before, but have picked them up again and continued to hold on to them. Let them cry out to You and admit that they are broken and need Your help. God please break the prideful spirit. God, I lift those up who are still hurting from childhood pains. God, I lift those up who are still hurting from bad relationships of the past and the present. God, I lift those up who are still grieving over a love one who have passed on. God, I lift up those who are hurting overall, and feel they have nowhere else to turn. God, I cast down any signs of depression or suicidal thoughts. God, I speak against any form of demonic thoughts that may be going through their minds right now. God right now I ask You to infuse them with the Holy Spirit. You O God will give them an inner peace that only You can give. God please just breathe on them, and reform their spirits from the inside out. God, I speak against a disobedient and rebellious spirit. God, I pray for a breakthrough and a release. God, You said in Your word that You would never leave or forsake us. God right now I speak from experience, there is a brighter day. I am living it right now!!!! God, You have been there for me through hell and high waters. God, You have helped me deal with childhood issues; generational curses; depression, insecurities, bad relationships, verbal abuse, and yes even suicidal thoughts as a teen. God, I thank You right now!!!!! You have always been there even when the devil tried to take me out through a love one. But God, I am still here and a witness that I overcame by Your grace and mercy. God my sisters and brothers can and will overcome. You are a God of peace, comfort and protection. God, I pray someone will change their path today and reach out to You. Give them the kind of peace that when they are alone, they are not lonely. Give them the kind of peace that when people speak nasty and untrue things about them, they don't think twice about it for they know who they belong to. God, You are AWESOME and I pray that each will truly come to know Your *awesomeness*. Every prayer that I prayed today God, I call it into existence. For someone will be set free. Amen!!! ***Flowing Strongly From Sarita's Pen.***

Keep Dancing Even If The Music Stops Playing

Inspired Thoughts . . .

We are creatures of habit. As long as the enjoyable music of life is playing, we dance. However, as soon as the music of life stops because of uncertain situations in life, we stop dancing. But I am here to tell you, keep dancing, because God will give you a song in your heart that is customized for you only. Sometimes you may even have to dance in the rain. Overcome and keep dancing.—*From Sarita's Pen.*

Scripture

Psalm 149:1-5 (NLT)

[1] Praise the Lord! Sing to the Lord a new song. Sing his praises in the assembly of the faithful. [2] O Israel, rejoice in your Maker. O people of Jerusalem,[a] exult in your King. [3] Praise his name with dancing, accompanied by tambourine and harp. [4] For the Lord delights in his people; he crowns the humble with victory. [5] Let the faithful rejoice that he honors them. Let them sing for joy as they lie on their beds.

Prayer

God, I come this morning with Psalm 34:1-5 (NLT) in my mouth. For it says "'I will praise the Lord at all times. I will constantly speak his praises. I will boast only in the Lord; let all who are helpless take heart. Come, let us tell of the Lord's greatness; let us exalt his name together. I prayed to the Lord, and he

answered me. He freed me from all my fears. Those who look to him for help will be radiant with joy; no shadow of shame will darken their faces." I thank You God for Your faithfulness. God, I pray for *the spirit of hallelujah anyhow.* No matter what is going on, I will continue to just be happy. I have learn to make the best of every situation and in due time, promotion and prosperity will come. In all that I do, I do it with a humble heart, and a bold spirit. God, I will keep dancing even if the music stops!!! Amen.
Flowing From Sarita's Heart & Pen

JUST BE YOU AND LOVE . . .
LIFE IS TOO SHORT

INSPIRED THOUGHTS . . .

I have learned in life to be 'just me'. You must be determined to be the woman or man God wants you to be. You can't let people dictate or take you out of your true character. Many times when people don't like you for any given reason, it is because deep down, they want to be you. But I say, when your haters give you hell, give them a hello, a smile, a goodbye, and speak blessings over them. Continue to be the loving person God intended you to be.—*From Sarita's Pen.*

SCRIPTURE

Matthew 5:44 (KJV)

But I say unto you, Love your enemies, bless them that curse you, do good to them that hate you, and pray for them which despitefully use you, and persecute you;

PRAYER

Thank You for my haters because they keep me on my toes. The storms causes me to appreciate the sunshine. The most important thing I thank You for is *The Word,* and the Holy Spirit that teaches me humility and how to handle the situations and my enemies. God, I pray today that we will grasp the concept that You will supply everything that is needed to handle our enemies and the people who don't like us just because of who we are and "who" we belong to. In 2 Corinthians 4:9 (NLT), it

tells us that we may be talked about and knocked down, but we are not destroyed because You, God, will never leave us. God, I appreciate and cling to the Apostle Paul's spirit of determination of not letting what people say or do keep me from helping others and moving into the destiny You have for me. God, I speak a word of encouragement and perseverance to those who are discouraged because of what "people say". Daniel 10:19 shows us that our words are powerful and can change the lives of people. I pray that each of us will encourage someone today and speak words of life. Encouragement is strength. In these times, it is not always easy to have a kind word in situations we are placed in, but God, I pray we will think before we speak not giving Satan any satisfaction of yielding to the temptation of using language that is not of You. I pray that we remember WWJD (What Would Jesus Do). A soft word will turn away wrath. Sometimes silence, a smile and walking away is the best way to irritate the enemy. Life is too short. Bless today, and I pray what You have given me will be a blessing to someone today and change a life. Amen!!!
Flowing From Sarita's Pen

CONTINUE TO GIVE THANKS . . . .
EVEN THROUGH DISTRACTIONS

INSPIRED THOUGHTS . . .

Never apologize for who you are and whose you are in Christ. Be who God designed you to be and always give thanks. Even more, let God be God and just LIVE!!! Your haters will soon get tired, or even better, God will move these distractions out of your life. Just walk into your season—**From Sarita's Pen**

SCRIPTURE

Psalm 136:16 (NLT)

Give thanks to him who led his people through the wilderness. His faithful love endures forever.

PRAYER

God, words can't express how I thank You for what You are doing in my life. Ephesians 5:20 (NLT) reminds us to give thanks for everything to God the Father in the name of our Lord Jesus Christ. God, I thank You for leading me through the wilderness. For only Your faithfulness and love will last. God, I pray for those who no one else is praying for. God this is a season of joy and happiness, but for some it is a season of depression. God bless those who suffer from depression. Give them the strength and the mindset of giving thanks for Your grace and mercy. Colossians 3:15 (NLT) tells us to let the peace that comes from Christ rule in our hearts. As members of one body, we are called to live in peace, and to always be thankful. God, I am thankful for the peace You have given and the godly people You have placed in my life. God, I am also aware of my enemies. I cast down every trick of the enemy in this season and speak death to his plots and distractions. *Today I say oh give thanks to the most high god.* You are worthy to be praised. Times are tough, and it seems that evil is everywhere. BUT God, the enemy is defeated, and Jesus is still LORD. I feel like Psalm 30:12(NLT) that states: "that I might sing praises to You and not be silent. O Lord my God, I will give You thanks forever!" Amen. **Flowing From Sarita's Heart & Pen**

Desirable and Winning Relationships

Inspired Thoughts . . . .

We all desire to have and be in loving and right relationships with family, friends, and significant others. But as I see more and more today, there is a strain on these relationships. There is so much discord, and many people are angry, hurt, bitter, insecure, and lack trust. There are many reasons why people behave the way they do in relationships. Nevertheless, in order for your relationships to be right and good, you must learn to be at peace with *you*. If you are not, then you are setting yourself up for failure. Most unhappy people always find something wrong with someone else BUT themselves. But one thing I learned over the years is that when you surrender yourself to God and establish a relationship with him first, all other relationships will fall in line. This requires alone time with Him through reading and studying His word, and prayer. God will show you *you*. He will give you peace, and all the anger, hurt, insecurities, and mistrust will soon diminish. It is not an overnight process nor is it easy. But once you find out who you are and whose you are in Christ, you become secure in yourself. You will become more at ease with others to establish or reconcile the loving and fulfilling relationships that every human being desires.—**From Sarita's Pen.**

Scripture

Luke 12:21 (NLT)

Yes, a person is a fool to store up earthly wealth but not have a rich relationship with God.

Exodus 34:14 (NLT)

You must worship no other gods, for the Lord, whose very name is Jealous, is a God who is jealous about his relationship with you.

<u>PRAYER</u>

Loving and always faithful God, I thank You today and yesterday for this topic on relationships. God, You know today the discord and issues with Your people. LORD, I speak blessings and peace into the air. Help each of us to understand that every successful relationship starts with You. God, I pray that we will surrender to You and Your will. God, I pray that we will not get caught up in the world and participate in what everyone else is doing especially if it is not of You. We, Your people are to be distinctive. Guide our footsteps and our tongue to speak positive things into the lives of our family and friends. God, I cast down jealously, envy, and all forms of malice. God, I pray that each will realize that the right relationship with You will foster the right relationship with everyone else. Luke 12:21 tells us that a person is a fool to store up earthly wealth but not have a rich relationship with You. We will not be foolish people. Having a right relationship with You will bring favor upon our lives, and windows of blessings will be upon to those who are subservient. Thank You God for this word today, and I am confident that someone will receive it and be blessed. Amen! **Flowing From Sarita's Pen.**

To My Beautiful Sisters in Christ: You Are a Gift!!!

Being a Christian is not easy especially being a Christian woman. There are many vices that work against you particularly if you are beautiful on the inside and the outside. Be careful, Satan will slither his way into your thoughts, and will attempt to make you believe your beauty is a curse. He may even try to attack you with depression. But I tell you this, God made you a blessing. Keep your head up, and press on in all your beauty. Keep praying, loving, uplifting, and smiling. God loves your joy, your smile, and your laughter. It makes Him smile. Pleasing God is all that matters.—**From Sarita's Pen**

Scripture

1 Peter 3:4 (NLT)

You should clothe yourselves instead with the beauty that comes from within, the unfading beauty of a gentle and quiet spirit, which is so precious to God.

2 Corinthians 4:16 (NLT)

That is why we never give up. Though our bodies are dying, our spirits are being renewed every day.

Galatians 6:9 (NLT)

So let's not get tired of doing what is good. At just the right time we will reap a harvest of blessing if we don't give up.

PRAYER

God, I thank You for all the encouraging words that I received these last few weeks. I know it was You who sent these angels in my life. Lord it gets hard sometimes. The more I try to live and do according to Your will, the more difficult it becomes. I know the higher the level, the greater the devils. But God, You always make a way and have equipped me to handle the situations. God, today I pray for my sisters in Christ who are not only beautiful on the outside, but the inside as well. In the name of Jesus, I bind and cast down every form of depression, every thought of suicide, and every misconception that the enemy will try to use to attack my sisters. When the enemy comes knocking at our door, give us the strength to tell him that we are not available to sin today. God, I pray that my sisters will not let any weapon slow them down. I pray a covering over them from the crown of their heads to the sole of their feet. I pray that my sisters will walk in humility, but continue to be bold for the LORD. Psalm 69:32 tell us that the humble will see God at work and be glad. Let all who seek God's help be encouraged. I pray that each will recognize that they are a special gift to the life of others even when it does not seem that way. I pray that my sisters will come to know *their worth*. It does not matter what the world says. It's what God says and that each of us believes what He says. Proverbs 31:10 (NLT) says that a virtuous woman worth is far above rubies, and that she is priceless. Thank You God for Your word, witnesses, and faithfulness. Amen. ***Flowing From Sarita's Pen***

IGNORANCE, STUPIDITY, OR BOTH?

INSPIRED THOUGHTS . . . .

In life you must deal with many things including ignorant people. There is no way around it. These people lack in knowledge or training, or in general "unlearned". Now if the truth is told, I believe in many cases it is more of stupidity and not ignorance. Stupidity is just clearly being foolish, unwise and having a dull mind. In essence, one knows what is right, but elects not to do right. The solution to ignorance can be resolved with just being informed or educated. Now, if ignorant people do not take advantage of the many free resources available to educate themselves in every area of their lives, they have moved from the state of ignorance to stupidity. They now know how, but they *decide* not. And just for the record, stupidity is present in every class; the poor, middle class, and yes, even the elite. The main goal for all is to utilize the resources that are available. Many times as Christians, we know better, but we opt to not do better. But just remember, at the end of the day, you are accountable for *you*. Now that you have been informed, if you are hanging around people in these two categories (ignorance and stupidity) who are ok being in their present state of *nothingness*, I suggest you change friends. Being affiliated with people of this nature is not wise no matter what side of the tracks you live on. Don't let anyone hold you back. ***From Sarita's Pen.***

SCRIPTURE

Hosea 4:6 (NKJV)

My people are destroyed for lack of knowledge. Because thou hast rejected knowledge, I will also reject thee, that thou shalt be no priest to Me. Seeing thou hast forgotten the law of thy God, I will also forget thy children.

Romans 10:3 (KJV)

For they being ignorant of God's righteousness, and going about to establish their own righteousness, have not submitted themselves unto the righteousness of God.

PRAYER

Father God, I come boldly before Your throne of grace thanking You for all Your goodness and mercy You have shown towards me. There is none like You O God my friend, my redeemer, and my ALL. God, I will never forget what You have done for me. I know that I am abundantly blessed. You have nothing but thoughts of love for me, therefore I know You want all of me. God continue to breathe into me Your breath of life. For Lo, I know You are with me. Just to be in Your presence is a beautiful thing. For everything that I have gone through, You told me in Your word that this too shall pass. God, I will continue to follow You all the days of my life. God, You have been just that good to me. You are my God and awesome is Your name!!!! You have told me many times that success is in your hand if I continue to seek You first. I know that You are a promise keeper, and I am covered. God bless every person reading this prayer and bless them in EVERY area of their life. God, I pray that each will grow in Your grace and mercy and become that woman and man You intend for each of us to be no matter what stage we are in our walk with You. This includes the babe in Christ to the seasoned Christians. Let the words of my mouth and the meditation of my heart be acceptable in your sight. Amen!!! *Flowing from Sarita's Heart & Pen.*

Don't Judge: Being Self-righteous is NOT Attractive

Inspired Thoughts . . . .

We all are still a work in progress. Just because you found Jesus today does not make you better than your buddies you were running with yesterday who have not surrendered to Christ. Sometimes, we forget so quickly where we came from and the life we once lived. Life is about choices. Sometimes we make the wrong choices, and we must to deal with the consequences. The right thing to do is to learn from your mistakes, and try not to repeat them. Pass on what you learned from your mistakes to the younger generation and stop putting your mouth on them in a negative way. Being self-righteous is not right. It is hypercritical.—*From Sarita's Pen*

Many times in life, we judge others situations according to our beliefs of 'why' things may have happened or not happened to that person. If a bad thing happened to someone, it is thought that they must have done something wrong or not pleasing to God. This is not always true. Just look at Job in the Bible. He was an upright man (Job 1:1). It rains on the just as well as the unjust. In everything that happens, God has a plan just for that situation. God ways are not like mans. He can take one situation and change millions of lives in a blink of an eye. Stop looking at every situation through the eyes of man. Start trying to look at it through the eyes of God. The Holy Spirit will guide you through this process.—*From Sarita's Pen.*

SCRIPTURE

Romans 3:23

for all have sinned and come short of the glory of God,

John 8:7

So when they continued asking Him, He lifted Himself up and said unto them, "He that is without sin among you, let him first cast a stone at her."

James 4:11 (NLT)

Don't speak evil against each other, dear brothers and sisters. If you criticize and judge each other, then you are criticizing and judging God's law. But your job is to obey the law, not to judge whether it applies to you."

PRAYER

God today, I come boldly before Your throne of grace thanking You for being God. God, I speak blessings and peace into atmosphere. Build up my sisters and brothers where they have a need, and restore them in every area of their lives. Where there is sickness, I pray healing. God where there is an addiction, I pray and proclaim that this stronghold will be broken in the name of Jesus. Where there are financial issues, I pray for financial increase. Where there are broken hearts, I pray that You put them back together again for You are the master potter. 1 Corinthians 13:7 tells us that love never gives up, never loses faith, is always hopeful, and endures through every circumstance. I cast down fear and desperation. Psalm 118:6(NLT) states: "The Lord is for me, so I will have no fear. What can mere people do to me?" God, I pray that every trap or weapon of destruction that the enemy has set will be uncovered and destroyed. God, he has no place or power, and we as Your children will not give him the satisfaction to cause havoc in our lives. We must be reminded of Ephesians 6:12 (NLT) that states: "For we wrestle not against flesh and blood, but against principalities, against powers, against the rulers of the darkness of this world, against spiritual wickedness in high places." But the key to fighting is as stated in Ephesians 6:10-18. We must be strong in the Lord and in his mighty power. We must put on all of God's armor so that we will be able to stand firm against all strategies of the devil. We are not fighting against flesh and blood enemies, but against evil rulers and authorities of the unseen world, against mighty powers in this dark world, and against evil spirits in the heavenly places. Therefore we must put on every piece of God's armor so we will be able to resist the enemy in the time of evil. Then after the battle we will still be standing firm. We must stand our ground, putting on the belt of truth and the body armor of God's righteousness. For shoes, put on the peace that comes from the Good News so that we will be fully prepared. In addition to all of these, hold up the shield of faith to stop the fiery arrows of the devil. We must put on salvation as our helmet, and take the sword of the Spirit, which is the word of God. We must always pray in the Spirit at all times and on every occasion. Stay alert and be persistent in our prayers for all believers everywhere. God, You are and have equipped each of us to handle what the enemy throws our way. God, I thank You for these weapons of warfare. We stand fighting the enemy, and knowing in the end that we have already won. We won the war over 2000 years ago on a hill called Calvary. God everything that has been spoken, I pronounce it and declare it done in Jesus name. It is so!!!!! Amen! ***Flowing From Sarita's Heart***

Strength From Struggles

Inspired Thoughts

We all have experienced the spirit of hopelessness when we are going through our trials. It is then that you must check your spiritual connection cord to God to make sure that it's fully plugged in and not totally unplugged. For your best life, stay focused and stay connected to your source. God is always there when man lets you down—***From Sarita's Pen***

Scripture

1 Peter 4:12-13 (NLT)

Dear friends, don't be surprised at the fiery trials you are going through, as if something strange were happening to you. Instead, be very glad—for these trials make you partners with Christ in his suffering, so that you will have the wonderful joy of seeing his glory when it is revealed to all the world.

Prayer

God, I thank You for my desert place. The desert place is where I will be given my instructions for Your kingdom. God, I thank You for Your peace. For having *internal peace* is power. Knowing who You are and whose You are is power. God, I thank You for the refiner's fire. Fire purifies the soul and burns away all the excess garbage. God, I thank You for protection. I speak blessings into the lives of those who pray this prayer. Bless them and protect them from the traps and tricks of the enemy as they walk in Your will and Your way. Let them know that You are God and will not put more on them than they can endure. Let them move into the area of blessing others while You are working out their issues. God give them the strength and the will to push on. Galatians 6:9 (NLT) states "And let us not be weary in well doing: for in due season we shall reap, if we faint not." God, I thank You for mercy and grace that You give daily. We calm victory for the war has already been won over 2000 years ago. IT IS SO! Amen. **Flowing From Sarita's Heart & Pen**

BE BOLD . . . . BUT HUMBLE

INSPIRED THOUGHTS

In today's society, many perceive the act of humility as a sign of weakness. For this reason, many people find it difficult to humble themselves. I have found in my short years here on earth that being humble has produced better results than being overly assertive. Humility is not humiliation. But not all can say or feel this especially if they don't know who they are in Christ. If you are confident in who you are in Christ, you won't *sweat the small stuff.* You can also walk in boldness at the same time. You may ask how this can be. The key is balance. Balance is something many of us today do not have in our lives. We either have the 'blow with the wind' mentality or the 'extreme' structured life. There is no balance on the measuring scale. This is not easy and it takes much practice with prayer, worship and praise. This means action is required, and something must be done. If one does not stand for something, he will fall for almost anything. Boldness requires confidence, and so does the practice of humility.—*From Sarita's Pen.*

SCRIPTURES

Proverbs 22:4 (KJV)

By humility and the fear of the LORD are riches, and honor, and life

Proverbs 29:23 (NLT)

Pride ends in humiliation while humility brings honor.

1 Peter 5:6 (KJV)

Humble yourselves therefore under the mighty hand of God, that he may exalt you in due time:

<u>PRAYER</u>

Good morning God. I come *boldly* before Your throne of grace this morning thanking You for just being God. I thank You for another day, another chance, and for being blessed and a blessing. God, I thank You for supplying all my needs. I thank You for equipping me to handle many of life's situations that come my way. God, I thank You even more for forgiving me when I messed up and not handling things the way I should have. This walk is not always easy. Thank You for not giving me what I deserve. Your grace and mercy covers it all. God bless every person praying this prayer with me today. God, I pray today for clarity in all of our lives. God many times we are confused about many things in life and our lives are out of balance. We as Christian try to live in the world and of the world, and this is when confusion comes in. God Proverbs 22:1-5 (NLT) tells us to "Choose a good reputation over great riches; being held in high esteem is better than silver or gold. The rich and poor have this in common: The Lord made them both. A prudent person foresees danger and takes precautions. The simpleton goes blindly on and suffers the consequences. True humility and fear of the Lord lead to riches, honor, and long life. Corrupt people walk a thorny, treacherous road; whoever values life will avoid it." God, I thank You for being an *all knowing* God, and snatching me out of situations before any damage can be done to me or my love ones. I pray that each will seek Your face in the areas of humility and boldness in Christ. You are always here God just waiting for each to reach out to You. God, I proclaim long life, peace, power, protection and prosperity. IT IS SO! Amen.—***Flowing From Sarita's Heart & Pen***

Beware of Book Cover Judgment

Inspired Thoughts

My sisters and brothers never look at the outer appearance only. There is a saying that everything that glitters is not always gold. Sometimes it's 'fool's gold' and you play the fool. Look at the heart as well. There is nothing more beautiful than a person who has inner beauty as well as outer beauty. For these individuals are priceless.—*From Sarita's Pen*

Scripture

James 2:1-9 (NKJV)

[1] My brethren, do not hold the faith of our Lord Jesus Christ, the Lord of glory, with partiality. [2] For if there should come into your assembly a man with gold rings, in fine apparel, and there should also come in a poor man in filthy clothes, [3] and you pay attention to the one wearing the fine clothes and say to him, "You sit here in a good place," and say to the poor man, "You stand there," or, "Sit here at my footstool," [4] have you not shown partiality among yourselves, and become judges with evil thoughts?[5] Listen, my beloved brethren: Has God not chosen the poor of this world to be rich in faith and heirs of the kingdom which He promised to those who love Him? [6] But you have dishonored the poor man. Do not the rich oppress you and drag you into the courts? [7] Do they not blaspheme that noble name by which you are called?

[8] If you really fulfill the royal law according to the Scripture, "You shall love your neighbor as yourself,"[a] you do well; [9] but if you show partiality, you commit sin, and are convicted by the law as transgressors.

PRAYER

God, I come boldly before Your throne of grace thanking You for grace, mercy, and favor!!!!! I thank You for not giving me what I deserve. Forgive me of my sins as I forgive those who have sinned against me. No words can express your goodness. I pray for every person reading this prayer. Bless them with peace, power, protection and prosperity. God, I pray for those no one else is praying for. God, I pray that all will renew or strengthen their relationship with you. You are the source of all our strength no matter what some may think or believe. It is in You that we have our being. God, I come praying that we not judge our sisters and brothers. For Luke 6:37 (NLT) states: "Do not judge others, and you will not be judged. Do not condemn others, or it will all come back against you. Forgive others, and you will be forgiven." God, I cast down the spirit of self-righteous. For Romans 3:23 tell us that we all have sinned and fallen short of Your glory. I cast down the spirit of negativity and I ask you to reveal the source in our lives that maybe causing the drama and confusion. I pray that when You do uncover the source, that we will make the right decision to remove these people out of our lives. God, I also pray that if You remove them, please improve them as well so they will not cause havoc in others' lives. God right now there is no time for this type of behavior. God, I pray that all will focus on their relationship with You as we live in these last days. I know that you will move in a mighty way and someone will be blessed, and You will receive the glory. God, I pray that each one of us will allow ourselves to continue to grow in You. I pray that each will take the limits off as it relates to You. For all things are possible with you. Thank you. Amen. **Flowing From Sarita's Heart & Pen**

Relationships: Don't Be A Prisoner of Your Own Insecurities

God has a new beginning waiting for you, but you must let go of the past. Don't let the enemy keep you in your present state. God will not allow one door to close without opening another one for you. When the devil reminds you of your past, you remind him of his future—**From Sarita's Pen**

Scripture

Proverbs 3:5-7(NLT)

5 Trust in the Lord with all your heart; do not depend on your own understanding. 6 Seek his will in all you do, and he will show you which path to take. 7 Don't be impressed with your own wisdom. Instead, fear the Lord and turn away from evil

Prayer

Father, I come boldly before your throne of grace thanking You for another day and another chance to live for You and try to get it right. God, I thank You for life, love, peace, happiness, and yes even my enemies who keep me on my toes and keep me humble. Lord, I speak blessings into every person's life who decided to take time to read this prayer. God, I pray that it blesses them far beyond anything they could ever think of or imagine. God, I feel and see that we are not progressing in life because we don't truly know You and also because we have let man pollute our thought process. God, I pray that each of us will move to the place in our lives where we will realize that YOU are the source of everything that is good and just. You, God can and will bless us in every area of our lives IF we would submit to You. I pray that we move from religion to relationship. God, I pray that we will wake up and become more aware of exactly what is going on in our world. It appears that our world is going to hell. BUT GOD!!!! You tell us in John 16:33 (NLT) that you have already overcome the world. The war has already been won. As Christians we must stay focus, recognize and cast down every distraction of the enemy. God, I thank You for continuing to open my eyes to the vices of the adversary. Because the higher we go in You, the stronger and more strategic the enemy becomes in his attacks. Many times he works within us, and before we know it, we become prisoners of our insecurities. God, I come praying for those that suffer from mental illness and are still in denial. God, I pray today that each of us will stop and take an assessment of our lives. You said that you would never leave us. You are good and your mercy and grace endures forever. Your word tells us that only what we do for Christ will last. Thank You!!!!! God, I speak blessings and a covering over all. Amen!!! **Flowing "Humbly" From Sarita's Heart & Pen.**

Relationships: Stay On Your Face 2 B N God's Face

Strive to improve and build your relationship with God first, and you will see miracles take place in other relationships. I'm just speaking from experience.—*From Sarita's Pen*

Scripture

Nehemiah 8:6 (NLT)

[6] Then Ezra praised the Lord, the great God, and all the people chanted, "Amen! Amen!" as they lifted their hands. Then they bowed down and worshiped the Lord with their faces to the ground

Prayer

LORD, I thank You for direction, protection, peace, and power. Thank You for Your never ending flow of Your word. The purpose of Your Word is to improve, increase, and empower Your people to move into being mature Christians. God, as I seek Your face in every area of my life, continue to infuse me with the light of the Holy Spirit. God, I pray to be taken to the next level, not for my glory, but for Your glory. I seek to be the best me You would have me to be, and to be a blessing to others. It's not about me, but about serving others with humility. We all are blessed to be a blessing. I pray for strength in times of weakness. I pray for peace in the middle of storms. God, I pray for clarity in times of confusion. But God most of all, I pray that each of us will form and strengthen our relationship with You. God, we are living in crucial times and every solder is needed to fight the enemy as he schemes to destroy all he encounters. God, time is out for AWOL (absent without leave) Christians. God, I pray for accountability in the body of Christ. If Christians don't stand for something, each of us will fall for anything. Lord thank You for Your blessings, grace, mercy, and all that You have done, are doing, and will do. I love You as I mature in moving from religion to relationship. Amen!—***Flowing from Sarita's Heart & Pen.***

Yes You Can Handle The Irritants Of Life!!!

<u>Inspired Thoughts . . . .</u>

Irritants are important in life. A pearl would not be a pearl without irritants. Irritations of life make you stronger and can even transform you into someone beautiful. Take life as it comes. Walk in Kingdom faith and listen to God when he speaks. Be ready to move when he says move. Get passionate about life and be who you say you are called to be having *no* fear. God has not given you the spirit of fear. IF you want your life to change for the better, do something different. Now is the time!!!!!—***From Sarita's Pen***

<u>Scripture</u>

John 16:33 (NLT)

33 I have told you all this so that you may have peace in me. Here on earth you will have many trials and sorrows. But take heart, because I have overcome the world."

Jeremiah 29:11(NLT)

11 For I know the plans I have for you," says the Lord. "They are plans for good and not for disaster, to give you a future and a hope

PRAYER

God today and every day is a special day. It is special because You made it and we live to see it. God, thank You for storms in my life because I now see they are serving a purpose. Thank You for the prophets who have spoken on the things that *are* coming to pass! Thank You for being patient with me and loving me. Forgive me for my sins as I forgive those who sinned against me. God today I say a special prayer for those who are true and ready to receive and move into what You have for them. I speak clarity into their lives. I speak that they will have the courage and power to walk away and cut the individuals out of their lives who are holding them back. Lord it is a hard thing to do sometimes, but LORD, we should love You more and want to be pleasing to You and not to man. I am a witness that You will bring new friends in our lives who are on the same page. God open doors today and make things clear for Your people who have been praying for a long time on the next steps to take. Today O my God, You will show up and they will know that it is You. Speak LORD!!! As Your servant, I am excited for everyone who is patient, faithful, believe, and obey You. The devil can't stop Your work. All the undercover demons on assignment will be revealed. When this happens, give Your people the strength to deal with disappoints and hurts. I pray that each will move on, and never look back. God, we live in the present, and moving toward the destiny You have for each of us. We are leaving the past behind. God thank You for *something different*, but most importantly thank You for blessing me to be a blessing. Amen!!! ***Flowing From Sarita's Heart & Pen***

GET TO KNOW YOU!!!

With guidance from the Holy Spirit, I truly became aware of me. It was then that it became a little easier for me to forgive, understand, trust, and love others—*From Sarita's Pen.*

SCRIPTURE

1 John 4:4 (NLT)

4 But you belong to God, my dear children. You have already won a victory over those people, because the Spirit who lives in you is greater than the spirit who lives in the world.

PRAYER

God, I thank You for Your faithfulness. Thank You for breathing into me life daily. I am humbled that You found me worthy to walk in spiritual authority and favor. I am a witness that you don't call the qualified, but qualify the called!! I bless all reading this prayer right now. God, I speak life into their lives and a word of encouragement to press on no matter what man may forecast. You are the author and finisher of our fate. God, I pray that we come to *truly* know who we are in You. When we move to become right in and with You, it is then all other relationships will fall into place. God, I forgive all of those who have attacked and wronged me. Bless those who have come back and apologize and even bless those who have not had the heart to do so. I realize that I must truly forgive those so that I will be forgiven for my transgressions, and move forward. God, I have learned at the end of the day, it is not about me, but about what is right in Your eyes. God, sometimes I find it hard to forgive my brothers and sisters because of hurt or just pride. But your word tells me in Proverbs 16:18 that pride goes before destruction and haughtiness before a fall. God, I also pray to move with speed from religion to relationship with You. Being religious can be dangerous to your people. It's easy to become distracted with things that are not of You. God, I pray with all my heart that your people will come to know who and whose they are. The enemy desires to keep us in ignorance so that he can continue to lead us astray with things that look holy but in reality are leading us down the pathway to hell. Continue to perform the miracles today as you did thousands of years ago. Open our blinded eyes and unstop death ears in the spirit. Bless today and move in a mighty way. This is my prayer for *each one* reading this prayer. Amen!!! ***Flowing From Sarita's Heart & Pen.***

Be A 'True' Friend to Have A 'True' Friend

Inspired Thoughts

A true friend will tell you what you *need* to hear, and not what you want to hear—***From Sarita's Pen***

Scripture

Proverbs 18:24 (NKJV)

[24]A man that hath friends must show himself friendly, and there is a friend that sticketh closer than a brother.

Prayer

God all I can say is Thank You!!! Thank You for new mercies and blessings I see daily. Thank you for being my friend. I know that I have a friend in You. You always look out for me and, take care of me. You tell and show me what I need to hear and see no matter how hurtful it may be. I know God that You have my best interest at heart. I know that You love me. Bless today and open eyes so that each of us will see and accept You in every area of our lives. God, I thank You for showing me *true love* and true *friendship*. Because you have been my guide, I am learning more and more daily about *true* friendship. Because of who you are, I give you glory. Because of who you are, I give you praise. Your faithfulness is priceless!!!!! Adoration belongs to you. I pray that not only the words of my mouth and the meditation of my heart be acceptable in your sight, but that these words change and reform relationships and lives. Amen!!—***Flowing from Sarita's Heart & Pen.***

LET HIM TALK TO YOU

INSPIRED THOUGHTS . . . .

God is speaking to us daily. He speaks through nature. He speaks through other people. He speaks in situations. He speaks directly to us through the Holy Spirit. However, sometimes we become distracted with unproductive things we place before him. In some cases, we catch a case of *selective hearing*. Be on alert, God is speaking to you. Let him to talk to you and be prepared to act on his word.—***From Sarita's Pen.***

Some find it difficult to pray. They feel a need to use special words or spiritual words in prayer. Just think of praying as having a conversation with God. He understands all languages, and he hears you. God wants and yearns for you to talk to him. He will answer you, but you have to remove the noise out of your life to hear him. Listening is the key to your spiritual growth.—***From Sarita's Pen***

SCRIPTURE

Job 33:14 (NLT)

For God speaks again and again, though people do not recognize it.

Mark 4:23 (NLT)

If any man have ears to hear, let him hear

PRAYER

God thank You for new revelation. God, I thank You for being there when no one else is there. You said in Your word that You would never leave or forsake us. God, thank You for letting me know that now is not the time to do nothing. NOW is the time God to live and not die . . . . NOW is the time to fight and not give up. Your word states that we fight not against flesh and blood but against spiritual wickedness in high places. I am also reminded in Your word that I can do all things through You God. You have not given me the spirit of fear, but of a sound mind. God, You remind me once again that Jesus has already overcome sin. We have to just live and seek first Your Kingdom. God, I thank You for peace today, and I know that You have equipped me with all that I need. God, I thank You for placing the right people in my life. These are the people who bless me. God, I pray to bless them even more. God, I thank You for letting me walk in my 'It'. God, I thank You for re-establishing me. I look forward to being that servant You would have me to be walking in humility and boldness at the same time. God, I pray for those no one else is praying for, and I ask You to move in a mighty way concerning my sisters and brothers who are still stuck and don't know what to do. The word I have for them is to just live and listen for You to speak to them. Life is not easy, but You God have all the answers and with You there is nothing too hard. God, I thank You for my freedom not just in the natural, but in the spirit. No weapon that is formed against this freedom that You give me shall prosper. The weapon is DOA (dead on arrival). IT IS SO!!!! Amen!!!
Flowing From Sarita's Heart & Pen

EMBRACING YOUR GIFTS: YOU HAVE A DECISION TO MAKE

INSPIRED THOUGHTS . . . .

The time is now where each one of us must truly stop and think about our lives. Are we living out our purpose? Have we embraced the gifts God has blessed each with to help others? Or are we afraid to embrace these gifts because we are afraid of what man will say? Job 22:21 tells us that if we agree with God quickly, we will have peace and be truly blessed. Look inside of yourself and truly seek who you are and embrace the God given gifts. I am wittiness to Job 22:21. God will give you peace and MANY doors with open.—*From Sarita's Pen*

SCRIPTURE

¹ Corinthians 12: 1, 4-7 (NLT) Now, dear brothers and sisters, regarding your question about the special abilities the Spirit gives us. I don't want you to misunderstand this. ⁴ There are different kinds of spiritual gifts, but the same Spirit is the source of them all. ⁵ There are different kinds of service, but we serve the same Lord. ⁶ God works in different ways, but it is the same God who does the work in all of us. ⁷ A spiritual gift is given to each of us so we can help each other.

Job 22:21(NLT)

²¹ "Submit to God, and you will have peace; then things will go well for you

<u>PRAYER</u>

God today I pray that You move in a supernatural way. I pray that each will open their eyes and ears to see and hear You when You move. I thank You God for being Jehovah God. *The eternal self-existing one who keeps his covenant promises to his covenant people"*. Amen!!!—***Flowing From Sarita's Pen***

Embracing New Beginnings

Inspired Thoughts . . . .

On this journey, death is a part of life. Not just physical death, but in the spiritual realm also. Some things must die in order for you to receive new. Let things go that really do not matter so God can give you "The New". Go with the flow of God and not against his movement. "Be" who you are called to be. It's not always about the doing, but it is about just "being". God wants you to live a good life of health and wellness. Stand and live on God's spoken word. Think on the positive things in life because consistently thinking on the negative will go against all things that God has for you. Negative thinking will not only upset your spirit, but it will eventually distress your health. Live and not die. I choose life, will you?—**From Sarita's Pen**

Some can't let go of their past because it is comfortable. You must let go in order to grow.—**From Sarita' Pen**

SCRIPTURE

Romans 12:2 (NLT)

Don't copy the behavior and customs of this world, but let God transform you into a new person by changing the way you think. Then you will learn to know God's will for you, which is good and pleasing and perfect

2 Corinthians 5:17 (NLT)

This means that anyone who belongs to Christ has become a new person. The old life is gone; a new life has begun!

PRAYER

God, I thank You so much for second chances today. Thank You for Your spirit that nurture, corrects and lives in me. God, I thank You for placing people and true friends in my life that have my best interest at heart. Lord, remove the people out of my life that are a hindrance to me and Your kingdom. God, thank You for the gift of discernment so that I may see things from Your perspective and not my own. God thank You for Your word that says that I can do all things through You. Thank You for Ephesians 3:20 (NLT) that states "Now unto him that is able to do exceeding abundantly above all that we ask or think, according to the power that worketh in us". Thank You for Jude 1:24(NLT) that says "Now unto him that is able to keep You from falling and to present You faultless before the presence of his glory with exceeding joy". Thank You for the joy that You have given and the peace that lives within me. Help me to walk in obedience, and to make the decisions to not rebel against Your word and Your leadership. Today I proclaim a new beginning and seek to always strive to do better not just for me, but to be a blessing to others. IT IS SO! Amen. **Flowing From Sarita's Heart & Pen**

Authentic Love

The word *Love* is used so loosely these days. Do we really know what love is? No we truly do not. Authentic or real love is very rare these days. Authentic love is unrestricted. 1 Corinthians 13 (NLT) says is best. Love is patient and kind. Love is not jealous or boastful or proud or rude. It does not demand its own way. It is not irritable, and it keeps no record of being wronged. It does not rejoice about injustice but rejoices whenever the truth wins out. Love never gives up, never loses faith, is always hopeful, and endures through every circumstance.—*From Sarita's Pen*

With guidance from the Holy Spirit, I truly became aware of me. It was then that it became a little easier for me to forgive, understand, trust, and love others.—*From Sarita's Pen*

Scripture

1 John 4:8 (NLT)

But anyone who does not love does not know God, for God is love.

Luke 6:32 (NLT)

"If you love only those who love you, why should you get credit for that? Even sinners love those who love them!

Ephesians 5:28 (NLT)

In the same way, husbands ought to love their wives as they love their own bodies. For a man who loves his wife actually shows love for himself

PRAYER

God, I thank You today for loving me unconditionally. You look beyond my faults and see my needs. I know LORD that no one can love me like You do. God, I thank You for the brand new mercies I see daily. This day was not promised to me, but I am ever so grateful. Lord, this means I have another day to get it right. God, I pray for those no one else is praying for. Please meet them at their needs. God, I lift those up who are reading this prayer. God bless them to truly seek You and love others with that same love You give to us. God, I pray that we all perform self-examination on our hearts and just be real. Proverbs 8:17 lets us know that You love all who love You. And those who search for You will truly find You. I pray that all will seek You to find that kind of love and peace that is life changing. God move in a mighty way. AMEN—***Flowing From Sarita's Heart & Pen.***

IDENTITY CRISIS

One of the biggest mistakes we make is allowing society to define who we are. This strategically happens through TV, radio, music, social media, and yes sadly even in church. You must look a certain way. You must be a part of a certain group; You must drive a certain car and live in a certain house. You must do all these things in order to fit in society. Many who pursue these things without placing God first in their lives are truly miserable!!!. These are the individuals who shed the tears of unhappiness late at night when no one else is around. This is the trick of the enemy to keep you in bondage. The solution to this is to: Know YOU. Know YOUR strengths and weaknesses. Get to know YOU. Be real with YOU. Embrace YOU. Love YOU. Get to know GOD. Form a relationship with GOD. Embrace His word. Embrace the Holy Trinity. LOVE GOD. Lose YOUrself to Gain YOUrself. Embrace the New Man. Let who YOU are in Christ determine what YOU do. Speaking from experience, once you are free, you will never want to go back. It is a sentiment that can't be truly expressed in words. It is then that YOU can truly live life . . . . life more abundantly.—***From Sarita's Pen With A SMILE***

SCRIPTURE

Jeremiah 1:5 (NLT)

[5] "I knew you before I formed you in your mother's womb. Before you were born I set you apart and appointed you as my prophet to the nations."

1 John 3:9-10 (NLT)

Those who have been born into God's family do not make a practice of sinning, because God's life is in them. So they can't keep on sinning, because they are children of God. So now we can tell who are children of God and who are children of the devil. Anyone who does not live righteously and does not love other believers does not belong to God.

1 Peter 2:9 (NKJV)

But you are a chosen generation, a royal priesthood, a holy nation, His own special people, that you may proclaim the praises of Him who called you out of darkness into His marvelous light

PRAYER

Father God, I thank You for these words that You have given. I pray it continues to resonate throughout the many days ahead. God, I am praying for and claiming total transformation. God, I pray that eyes will be opened. God, I pray many will sober up from the drunkenness of society and man's grip on their lives. God, I proclaim freedom that many will experience the first time in their lives. Now, Satan we put You on notice that all Your tricks and distractions will fail. God, I pray for protection of the mind from Satan vices that he so cunningly try to use. Give each strength to walk according to Your will. No more excuses God. Now thank You for Your mercy and grace that is seen daily. IT IS SO!!!! Amen. ***Flowing From Sarita's Heart & Pen***

Power: The Power Within: Tap Into It

The Power of Words: Exercise Your Power w/ Control

Inspired Thoughts . . .

My tongue is my sword of power. I use it wisely. For today I will practice the art of silence and only speak under the authority of the Holy Spirit—**From Sarita's Pen**

Scripture

1 Peter 3:10 (NASB)

The one who desires life, to love and to see good days, must keep his tongue from evil and his lips from speaking deceit.

Prayer

Let the words of my mouth and the meditation of my heart be acceptable in Your sight God. God, today I thank You for *Your word* that guides me to make the right decisions in my life. Sometimes that does not always happen because I take a detour from *Your word* and use my own words. But through it all God, You always make a way. I learn from my mistakes. Lord bless today and I pray that we as Christians will think before we speak. Proverbs 18:21 tells us that life and death are in the power of the tongue. God give us a fresh anointing to do our jobs. God give me a fresh anointing to give Your people a word to bless them in their everyday lives. Thank You for the gift of today as we each should rejoice and be glad in it. Amen!!! **Flowing From Sarita's Pen.**

CLEAN YOUR HOUSE OF NEGATIVE INFLUENCE

INSPIRED THOUGHTS . . .

Sometimes our disobedience is connected with our sphere of influence. Be mindful of who you spend your time with.—*From Sarita's Pen*

SCRIPTURE

Psalm 138:7 (NLT)

Though I am surrounded by troubles, you will protect me from the anger of my enemies. You reach out your hand, and the power of your right hand saves me

Philippians 4:19 (KJV)

But my God shall supply all your needs according to his riches in glory by Christ Jesus.

Revelation 2:26 (KJV—21st Century)

And he that overcometh and keepeth My works unto the end, to him will I give power over the nations,

PRAYER

Father God, I thank You for life this morning. I thank You for waking me up in a sound mind. A mind focused on what I can do today to make someone's life better and to be a blessing.

Lord, I thank You today for giving me the spirit of boldness and not of fear. I thank You LORD for Your word and knowing that it is true. Lord I thank You for a reality check sometimes. Thank You for pushing me and shifting me into the position of where You want me to be and not where I want to be. Lord, I thank You for ticking me off and making me mad enough to do something about the situation. Lord, I thank You for covering and protecting me. Thank You for the unknown instructions. Instructions that didn't make sense to me, but when followed, You received the glory. God, continue to place the people in my life that are connected to my destiny and remove the people who are not. God, by the power that You have given me, I rebuke and bind every spirit that is not off You and every witch and every warlock on assignment to destroy Your kingdom. Lord, I pray that these destructive spirits in leadership and non-leadership roles will be exposed soon and destroyed. Lord, I pray that my sisters and brothers will walk in the gifts that You have given them not caring what the world may think. I pray that they will come to know You and have peace within themselves knowing that with You God all things are possible. God, I pray that when they come into the know, they will walk with their heads up high proclaiming that they belong to You. And not allowing the world make them believe they are any less. And also, LORD, let them walk this walk with humility. Lord, bless Your children with peace, power, protection and prosperity. I lift those up who may be unemployed at this time. Lord, let them hear Your voice as You order their steps on their next job assignment. Hebrews 13:5 tells us that You would never leave or forsake Your people. Lord, guide our footsteps and our tongues so when we speak, we speak under Your influence and not our own. For Your people in the workplace, give us a fresh anointing to do our jobs today as we strive to transform and set the tone. God, I thank You for strategically placing Your people in the workplace. Lord, let us not judge people because God You can use anyone to do Your work from the cleaning crew to the CEO. Lord forgive us of our sins as we forgive those who have sinned against us. Let us not

It's NOT Always About You. Get Over Yourself!!!

Inspired Thoughts . . .

If you don't stand for something, you will fall for anything. Stand for what you believe in and allow your past hurts, pains and tests in general be testimonies. On the other hand, you are not the only person that can think and possess life changing ideas. God made each one of us unique with gifts and talents that he can also use for his Kingdom. As a true Christian, being selfish or self-centered is not an option. You can't be heartless or selfish in your giving, living and forgiving. For you are blessed to be a blessing, and blessings do not always emerge in a material form.—**From Sarita's Pen**

Scripture

2 Corinthians 13:8 (NLT)

For we cannot oppose the truth, but must always stand for the truth.

Mark 11:25-26 (NLT)

But when you are praying, first forgive anyone you are holding a grudge against, so that your Father in heaven will forgive your sins, too."

Prayer

Father God, I thank You for life this morning. I am grateful for You waking me up in a sound mind and with my mind on what I can do today to make someone's life better. Lord, I thank You today for giving me the spirit of boldness and not of fear. I thank You LORD for Your word and knowing that it is true. Lord, I thank You for a reality check sometimes, and for pushing me and shifting me into the position of where You want me to be and not where I want to be. Lord I thank You for making me mad enough to do something about the situation. You said if I just trust you, You will take care of every situation that I may be dealing with. Lord, I thank You for covering and protecting me. God, continue to place the people in my life that are connected to my destiny and remove the people who are not and who form weapons against me. God, by the power that You have given me, I rebuke and bind every spirit that is not off You and every demon on assignment who tries to destroy Your kingdom. Lord, I pray that my sisters and brothers will walk in the gifts that You have given them not caring what the world may think. I declare and decree that they shall have peace in their storms; that they have the mind to tap into the power that You have infused them with; and they also have a prosperous mind set. I lift those up who maybe still unemployed at this time. Lord, let them hear Your voice as You order their steps on their next job assignment. In Your word (Hebrews 13:5) You state that You would never leave or forsake Your people. Lord, guide our footsteps and our tongues so when we speak, we speak under Your influence and not our own. For Your people in the workplace, give us a fresh anointing to do our jobs today as we strive to transform and set the tone. God, thank You for strategically placing Your people in the workplace. Lord, let us not judge people for You can use anyone to do Your work . . . from the cleaning crew to the CEO. Lord forgive us of our sins as we forgive those who sin against us. Let us not have a self-righteous attitude and walk in selfishness. God, I thank You for this time of reflection and every word that I have spoken, I decree it, declare it and call it into exists. IT IS SO! Amen—***From Sarita's Heart/ Pen***

BE WHO YOU ARE CALLED TO BE

Trust God in all that you do. Each of us has a mission no matter the magnitude. But be who <u>You</u> are called to be and <u>NOT</u> someone else.—*From Sarita's Pen*

SCRIPTURE

Psalm 56:4 (NLT)

I praise God for what he has promised. I trust in God, so why should I be afraid? What can mere mortals do to me?

PRAYER

God Your faithfulness never cease to amaze me. You hear me when I call out to You. You protect me from my enemies whose main purpose is to destroy me and my family. Your love is never ending. You give me strength in many forms; anywhere from music to the special people You place in my life. You are there when I make mistakes and You are there when I pass on blessings You have given me. You know me God like no one else. There is none like You. I believe in Your word in Jeremiah 29:11 (NLT) "For I know the plans I have for You, says the Lord. They are plans for good and not for disaster, to give You a future and a hope". Grant me the things that are needed, and I pray to continue to be faithful to You. Life will bring about some challenges, but God, You are the source of my being and my finances. You have made a way and I know You will continue to make a way. I see promotions and not poverty for Your people. Thank You for favor. No one God can love me like You do. They may come close, but You are the true lover of my soul. No one or nothing will come between us. The mission You have given me *will be* successful. IT IS SO! Amen. ***From Sarita's Heart & Pen***

YOU CAN'T STOP GOD'S WORK

INSPIRED THOUGHT

Satan can't stop God. The truth be told, Satan knows this. But this does not prevent him from trying. We as Christians give up at a blink of an eye. God made us in his image. He has given us power to handle the enemy. Satan knows this also because God made him. Read your bible!!! Satan was once an angel in heaven. He is known as the fallen angel. You could learn a lesson from Satan in perseverance. In essence, Satan knows the power of God, and it is a shame that many of God's children don't—***From Sarita's Pen***

SCRIPTURE

1 JOHN 4:4 (NLT)

But you belong to God, my dear children. You have already won a victory over those people, because the Spirit who lives in you is greater than the spirit who lives in the world.

Luke 10:19 (KJV)

Behold, I give unto you power to tread on serpents and scorpions, and over all the power of the enemy: and nothing shall by any means hurt you.

PRAYER

God, I pray Isaiah 54:17-18 (NLT) that states: "No weapon that is formed against thee (me) shall prosper; and every tongue that shall rise against thee (me) in judgment thou (You) shalt condemn. This is the heritage of the servants of the LORD, and their righteousness is of me, saith the LORD." This is Your word LORD and I am standing on Your word. I pray for others to believe and walk in it today. IT IS SO! Amen. **From Sarita's Heart & Pen**

Progress Check . . . .
Stop Wasting Time

Inspired Thoughts . . .

Work what God has given you. For God wants to bless you over and above what you can imagine. However, you can't truly be free to do this if you are letting a stubborn and rebellious spirit hold you back—**From Sarita's Pen**

Scripture

Isaiah 42:9 (KJV)

Behold, the former things are come to pass, and new things do I declare: before they spring forth I tell you of them.

Matthew 9:17 (KJV)

Neither do men put new wine into old bottles: else the bottles break, and the wine runneth out, and the bottles perish: but they put new wine into new bottles, and both are preserved.

Prayer

God thank You today for all Your blessings. Thank You for giving me what I need to move forward and focus on the purpose and not the problem. God, if we would only stay focus on the purpose and not be distracted, more could be accomplished. God, I pray for every person I come in contact with today. Bless each with what they need. God, I pray that each realize that time is precious, and we can't be selfish with it. Your time God is the most precious. God transform and re-focus minds on the purpose and not the problem. Problems have no power with You God in the middle of the situation. You have proven this time and time again. God, I rebuke procrastination and all the negative things that go with it. For I proclaim that failure is not an option in 2010. Amen!!! ***Flowing From Sarita's Heart & Pen***

A Change Agent: Your Circumstances Can Bless Others

Life happens is a phrase that we see or use a great deal. We deal with hurt, pains, and disappointments. But through it all, God will do what He promised. The one thing that you must do with your life circumstances is to utilize them to advance the gospel. Don't see these events as roadblocks. But see them as changes to expand the cause of Christ. You can be that change agent.— ***From Sarita's Pen***

Scripture

Romans 15:2 (NLT)

We should help others do what is right and build them up in the Lord.

1 Corinthians 12:28 (NLT)

Here are some of the parts God has appointed for the church: first are apostles, second are prophets, third are teachers, then those who do miracles, those who have the gift of healing, those who can help others, those who have the gift of leadership, those who speak in unknown languages.

Prayer

God, I thank You for 'My It'. Thank You for a clear vision of doing what You want me to do. For I know with You, I can do 'It'. God, I

pray that each one of us walk in and do our own personal 'It'. For the ones who are walking according to their 'It', I pray blessings over their lives, and continue to give them staying power to see their 'It. God we all can be change agents for You. Everyone has different assignments, and I pray that each will continue to focus on their assignments and not on others. God give the spirit of boldness to the ones who seek it, and cast out fear. God we will transform lives and help give birth to new beginnings. God, I pray that Your people will let You use them in the way You want to use them. Not all are destined to be in the spotlight. For every assignment is important and plays a major part in the kingdom. God, I speak a word of humility and peace into each ones spirit. God, I pray for more change agents in Your kingdom who have the right spirit and not one of self-gratification. God, it is time out for Christians to be quiet when they should speak up for You, and not be ashamed of their situations. God let us see our circumstances as blessings to others and not roadblocks. For what the devil intended for bad, You will turn into good. For with You God, there is no failure. I pray for clarity today and then I pray that all will take action once You speak to them. God, I pray that You will open the hearts and eyes of our African American men. God we need them like we have never needed them before for our children and for our communities. If anyone circumstances could be turned into blessings, it is the African American men. For the African American men who are going above and beyond, bless them with a supernatural blessing. Peace, power, protection, and prosperity are ours. It is so ! Amen.
Flowing From Sarita's Heart & Pen

I Am What He Says I Am. Just Believe It

I can pray for you all day long, but when are you going to start praying for yourself and believe in your own prayers? God is all powerful, he can listen, answer prayers, and save millions at the same time.—**From Sarita's Pen**

If you want your life to improve and go to the next level, you must surrender to the victory in you. You can do it, because it is already done. It is a process, but you must live for and in God. God lives in you. Stop complaining and whining, and take back what has been taken from you. In some situations take back what you freely gave the enemy under the wrong influence. Be proactive and not reactive. Walk in your authority and power and say to yourself every morning; "I belong to God, and he has given me the power to do all things and that means even kick the devils butt today".—**From Sarita's Pen**

Scripture

Ephesians 3:20 (NLT)

Now all glory to God, who is able, through his mighty power at work within us, to accomplish infinitely more than we might ask or think.

1 John 5:4 (NLT)

For every child of God defeats this evil world, and we achieve this victory through our faith.

PRAYER

First, thank You God for another day that was not promised. Thank You for new mercies I see this day. Thank You for infusing me with what I need daily to live life and to live life well in You. God, I thank You for placing the right people in my life. I thank You for blessing and moving in spite of me and others. God, I ask You to bless supernatural today. I pray Your people will truly hear You speak and believe. Believe and know that You have their lives in Your hands. I pray for that person who says they believe, but fail to walk into the promises You have showed them many times. Take away the excuses God and show them who You really are. As I look at the news daily, time is at hand and there is much to be done. God, I ask You to bless all the leaders. Give them strength to continue to work for You, and I ask You to continue to build them up to believe even more in Your glory. In the end God, You have the last say so. Victory is ours and the prince of darkness is defeated!!!! It is so! Amen! **Flowing From Sarita's Heart & Pen**

Mid-Year Check: Are U Pushing Forward or Looking Back?

Inspired Thoughts . . . .

We all set goals for our lives and vowed to work toward these goals in 2010. However, at the mid-point of 2010, we need to ask ourselves these questions: How am I progressing? How is my relationship with God? Am I where I should be? IF not, Why? We all have a reason for not being exactly where we should be. Nevertheless, as you travel on this journey, there are many things that must be taken into consideration. First, are you *speaking life* into your own life and others? You can kill a manifestation with your negative words. Many times I have heard that life and death are in the power of the tongue. Next, are you engaging in *God's Oneness*? Being and staying connected to and in God is the key to the success on this journey. Be and stay focus not letting anyone or anything throw you off course. Many people with good intentions will give you good advice BUT not *God advise*. It would be in your own best interest to lean the difference. You know what and how to do that.—**From Sarita's Pen**

Scripture

Philippians 3:12 (NLT)

I don't mean to say that I have already achieved these things or that I have already reached perfection. But I press on to possess that perfection for which Christ Jesus first possessed me

Philippians 3:14 (NLT)

I press on to reach the end of the race and receive the heavenly prize for which God, through Christ Jesus, is calling us.

<u>PRAYER</u>

To the only wise God my Savior. Thank You once again for moving right on time. Not when I desire, but in Your time. God, I look back over these last five months of 2010 and I say thank You. It has not been easy, but I am still here P.U.S.H. ing (Praying Until Something Happens). I pray that we live the life according to your will. I pray for greater peace, greater power, greater protection, and greater prosperity. We all are blessed regardless of everything going on in our lives. I know God that it could be worse. God, I pray for each and every person praying this prayer with me. I speak life into their lives and pray that each will start to speak positive things into their own lives. God, I pray that their hearts and eyes will open and know that you are there to comfort and supply their every need. God, I pray that each will PUSH forward and not look back. With you God, there are only good things ahead. I decree it, declare it and call it into existence by the power you have given me. It is so!!! Amen! ***Flowing From Sarita's Heart & Pen***

THIS TIME GET YOURSELF TOGETHER!!!

INSPIRED THOUGHTS

Today is new day and God has put some things in motion for you to do today. Don't worry, just follow his lead and he will do the rest. The key to this simple message is *take action*. As I have stated many times before, God will not always step out of heaven and do everything for you. He will provide you with everything that you need through his angels he assigns to you.—**From Sarita's Pen**

SCRIPTURE

1 John 5:4 (NLT)

For every child of God defeats this evil world, and we achieve this victory through our faith

PRAYER

God, I thank You for new revelation. God, I thank You for being there when no one else is there. You said in Your word that You would never leave or forsake me. God thank You for letting me know that now is not the time to do nothing. *Now* is the time God to live and not die. *Now* is the time to fight and not give up. Your word states that we fight not against flesh and blood but against spiritual wickedness in high places. I am also reminded in Your word that I can do all things through You God and You have not given me the spirit of fear, but of a sound mind. God, You remind me once again that Jesus has already overcome sin. We must live and seek first Your Kingdom. God, I thank You for peace today, and I know that You have equipped me with all that I need. God, I thank You for sending me to and placing the right people in my life. People who have rally blessed me. God, I thank You for letting me walk in my "It". God, I thank You for re-establishing me. I look forward to being that servant You would have me to be walking in humility and boldness at the same time. God, I pray for those no one else is praying for and ask You to move in a mighty way concerning my sisters and brothers who are still stuck and don't know what to do. The word I have for them is *to just live* and *listen* for You to speak. Life is not easy, but You God have all the answers and with You there is nothing too hard. God bless this day and this weekend as we celebrate "Independence Day". God, I thank You for my freedom not just in the natural, but in the spirit. No weapon that is formed against this "freedom" that You gave me shall prosper. For the weapon is DOA (dead on arrival). It is so! Amen!!! **Flowing From Sarita's Pen**

Strongholds: R U Breaking or Nurturing Them?

Inspired Thoughts . . .

Through the power of pray, I can break the devil's will over you. But I can't break your will over the devil. <u>You</u> must release him.— **From Sarita's Pen.**

Scripture

Romans 6:7-10 (NLT)

For when we died with Christ we were set free from the power of sin. [8] And since we died with Christ, we know we will also live with him. [9] We are sure of this because Christ was raised from the dead, and he will never die again. Death no longer has any power over him. [10] When he died, he died once to break the power of sin. But now that he lives, he lives for the glory of God.

Romans 6:12-14(NLT)

Do not let sin control the way you live; [a] do not give in to sinful desires. [13] Do not let any part of your body become an instrument of evil to serve sin. Instead, give yourselves completely to God, for you were dead, but now you have new life. So use your whole body as an instrument to do what is right for the glory of God. [14] Sin is no longer your master, for you no longer live under the requirements of the law. Instead, you live under the freedom of God's grace.

PRAYER

God, You are and have been an awesome and faithful God. God today I pray for those who are dealing with strongholds in their lives. God right now I pray that each will focus on the *God things* in life and not just the things of the world. There are so many distractions today. We can so easily get caught up and not even know we are caught up. God, I pray that each will take authority over their thoughts and bind all spirits of fantasy and any lustful thinking in the name of Jesus. God, I pray today for clarity for each in order that they may see and hear the difference between Your voice and the enemy's voice. God, I pray that You would grant the gift of discernment for those who are seeking it. God for those who are flowing in the gift, I pray that You elevate their gift to a higher level to even be more of a blessing to them as well as others. God, I pray today that the root of every stronghold is routed out to exist no more. It is so!!! Amen! ***Flowing From Sarita's Pen***

I Can Control Me If Nothing Else

Inspired Thoughts . . . .

I always remind my little girl that there are certain things in life you have no control over, but your mouth is the one thing that "YOU" can control. Never forget that.—*From Sarita's Pen*

Take charge of yourself first and not others. When you start trying to manipulate or control others, this is when you lose control of yourself. You are setting yourself up for failure.—*From Sarita's Pen.*

Scripture

Romans 8:6 (NLT)

So letting your sinful nature control your mind leads to death. But letting the Spirit control your mind leads to life and peace.

Romans 8:8 (NLT)

That's why those who are still under the control of their sinful nature can never please God

James 3:2 (NLT)

Indeed, we all make many mistakes. For if we could control our tongues, we would be perfect and could also control ourselves in every other way.

Sarita Price

PRAYER

Good afternoon Lord! Thank You for this day. Thank You for times when I can step back and reflect on the good and the bad. You blessed me to make it through the bad and celebrate all Your goodness in every area of my life. God today I come praying for a spirit of self-control. God help each to master self-first. God we all have developed habits that are irritating to You. Proverbs 5:23 tells us that each will die for lack of self-control, and will be lost because of our own great foolishness. Please help us to change that. We only want to have good habits. Psalm 141:3 also tells us to take control of what we say, O Lord, and guard our lips. God we want to do and say the right things so that we may be a blessing to You, to our family, to our friends, and everyone we meet. Please forgive us of our sins and failures. God today I commit to You, that with Your help, I will change for the better. I praise and worship You, Lord. Amen!!! ***Flowing From Sarita's Heart & Pen.***

ARMED AND DANGEROUS: ANNIHILATE YOUR OWN PERSONAL DEMONS IN ORDER TO OVERCOME AND LIVE

INSPIRED THOUGHTS . . .

I have discovered through reading, prayer, and life experiences that in order to overcome the small demons (lust, lying, fornication, adultery, stealing, cheating, backbiting, etc . . .), I must first annihilate the two master demons in which these small demons get their strength from. These two master demons are "insecurity" and "inferiority". Satan was very clever. He released these two demons in the Garden of Eden upon Adam and Eve (Eve especially), and they have been causing havoc from the beginning of time. But God has given each of us the power to overcome. It starts with seeking a relationship with Him and acknowledging daily that Jesus Christ is our Savior. Once you know who you are in Christ, and continue to cultivate your relationship with God, the devil in hell don't have a chance.— ***From Sarita's Pen.***

SCRIPTURE

Ephesians 3:20 (NIRV)

God is able to do far more than we could ever ask for or imagine. He does everything by his power that is working in us.

PRAYER

Good morning God and thank You for another chance to share and bless someone today. God today I pray with strength and power that the word that is going forth today will be a blessing to someone. God, I pray that each will truly perform a self-examination and uncover the true source that is causing all the confusion in their lives. God create in us a clean heart and renew in each Your Spirit. I pray that each will continue to fight and not give up. The enemy is crafty, and he personalizes his attacks. We all have different temptations and what may cause a downfall for one may not affect another. Satan knows the flavor that each one desires. God right now I come against the spirit of "insecurity" by speaking words of self-confidence and self-assurance. For 1 Chronicles 16:11 states "Search for the Lord and for his strength; continually seek him. 1 Corinthians 4:20 also tells us "For the Kingdom of God is not just a lot of talk; it is living by God's power." I come against the spirit of "inferiority" by speaking words of advantage and dominance. Deuteronomy 28:13 states "If you listen to these commands of the Lord Your God that I am giving you today, and if you carefully obey them, the Lord will make you the head and not the tail, and you will always be on top and never at the bottom". God, I pray that each of us will let Your word take root in their minds and stop living beneath our privileges. For we are worth so much more than what man says we are. God, I pray that each of us will act upon the power and the authority that You have given us. But God You gave each of us a will and it is up to each to follow the right path. The path YOU have placed before us. Amen!!! ***Flowing From Sarita's Heart & Pen.***

R U Going to Sit Back and Let the Devil Kick Your Butt????

Inspired Thoughts . . .

You know it's a little distressing to see Christians today just let the enemy run all over them while they sit back, cry, and just quote scriptures like Isaiah 54:17 with NO power. You have to speak Gods word with power, authority, and belief. Because if you don' believe what you say, what makes you think your enemies will believe you. Some of us have been in church all our lives and can quote almost every scripture from Genesis to Revelation in the Bible but still have no power. Another thing, stop letting people disrespect your dreams and goals. If this is what God has given you, learn how to laugh in the enemies face and say "nice try, but I'm covered". Get a backbone in the spirit and stop having a jelly back. Every chance I get, I remind the enemy of whose I am and the power God has given me through the Holy Spirit. I'm just trying to help you along the way.—**From Sarita's Pen**

Scripture

Luke 10:19 (NLT)

[19] Look, I have given you authority over all the power of the enemy, and you can walk among snakes and scorpions and crush them. Nothing will injure you

Romans 8:31 (KJV)

What shall we then say to these things? If God be for us, who can be against us?

PRAYER

God, You are the almighty God and I am Your child. Therefore, You have given me the power to speak to the enemy in the name of Jesus Christ and he will flee. I thank You Father for equipping me. Amen!!! ***Flowing From Sarita's Pen.***

DON'T LET YOUR WINTER STORMS SHUT YOU DOWN . . . . POWER UP!!!!!!

INSPIRED THOUGHTS . . .

Storms of life are just a part of living, and will appear in every season. Some may be harsher than others. Winter storms can sometimes be the worst. They can be hard, cold, impairing, blinding, and sometimes depressing. For a while, you may be stuck in one place, and you may even lose power. Just overall, your life is just depressing. But I challenge you that when the winter storm comes in your life, pull out your spiritual generator and connect to *The power source of God*. And if your generator is not working properly, hook up with other believers who encompass power. True believers are always willing to allow you to come into their homes, and share with you *the source* of their being. But be warned; don't let your pride keep you from seeking help. When winter storms come into your life, don't shut down. There is always t*he power source of God* available to warm your heart and spirit. 2 Corinthians 1:3 tells us that we owe all praises to God, the Father of our Lord Jesus Christ. God is our merciful Father and the source of all comfort. This source is not controlled by man and will never fail you.—*From Sarita's Pen.*

SCRIPTURE

2 Samuel 22:33 (KJV)

God, Is my strength and power: and he makes my way perfect.

Psalm 18:2 (NLT)

The Lord is my rock, my fortress, and my savior; my God is my rock, in whom I find protection. He is my shield, the power that saves me, and my place of safety.

PRAYER

Merciful God, I thank You for just being God. I thank You for Your word that ministers, heals, and continues to push me into greatness. Lord, You are my source and my strength. When things seem confusing and I am being attacked on every end, You are there guiding me. When my finances look funny and the pressures of the world seem heavy, You not only make a way, but overflow is present. God today I pray for those no one else is praying for. I pray for those that are going through and are at the end of their rope. God, I pray that they will tap into their power source The Comforter; The Holy Spirit. God manifest in each person life today. For those that are babes in Christ, make their way clear and guide them. For those who are more seasoned Christians, infused them with Your power. Take them to the next level in You so that they can truly be a blessing to Your Kingdom and a threat to the kingdom of darkness. God in Psalm 18:2 you remind me that You are my rock, my fortress, and my savior; and I find protection in You. You are my shield, the power that saves, and a place of safety. God thank You for sending people into my life who impact me, and push me to go on and live life well in You. Amen!!! ***Flowing From Sarita's Heart & Pen.***

Spiritual Authority
and Favor of God

Inspired Thoughts

Stand still and watch God work when your enemies try to destroy your self-esteem. Remember keep reading the word of God, praying and praising. Move with authority when God gives you instructions. Promotion comes not from man but GOD!!!. As you stand boldly as a child of the King, you need to tell your enemies this: "Back up off me. You have messed with the wrong Christian today!!!!"—*From Sarita's Pen*

Scripture

Luke 10:19 (NLT)

[19] Look, I have given you authority over all the power of the enemy, and you can walk among snakes and scorpions and crush them. Nothing will injure you.

Romans 8:31 (NLT)

What shall we say about such wonderful things as these? If God is for us, who can ever be against us?

Prayer

Thank You for my haters because they keep me on my toes, and the storms make me appreciate the sunshine. The most important thing I thank You for is Your word and the Holy Spirit that teaches me humility and how to handle the situations and my enemies. God, I pray today that each of us will grasp the concept that You will supply everything that is needed to handle our enemies and the people who don't like us just because of who we are and who we belong to. In 2 Corinthians 4:9, it tells us that we may be talked about and knocked down, but we are not destroyed because You God will never leave us. God, I appreciate and cling to the Apostle Paul's spirit of determination of not letting what people say or do keep me from helping others and moving into the destiny You have for me. God, I speak a word of encouragement and perseverance to those who are discouraged because of what people say. Daniel 10:19 shows us that our words are powerful and can change the lives of people. I pray that each of us will encourage someone today and speak words of life. Encouragement is strength. In these times, it is not always easy to have a kind word in situations we are placed in, but God, I pray that each of us will think before we speak not giving Satan any satisfaction of yielding to the temptation of using language that is not of You. I pray that we remember WWJD (What Would Jesus Do). A soft word will turn away wrath. Sometimes silence, a smile and walking away is the best way to irritate the enemy. Bless today and I pray that what You have given me will be a blessing to someone today and change a life. Amen ***Flowing From Sarita's Heart & Pen***

Do What You R Equipped To Do and Stand Still !!!!

Inspired Thoughts . . . .

Many of us are in a season where God is repositioning us. Put things in order and do what God has assigned and equipped you to do. Walk in your purpose, and trust God in your transition. There is value in *the promise* even in the toughest times. In this process, acknowledge and celebrate the small victories. Don't let the enemy hijack your joy, peace, and self-esteem. Stand on and believe Isaiah 54:17 (NLT) and watch Satan's plots and devices crash and burn!!!—*From Sarita's Pen*

Scripture

Nehemiah 6: 9, 11(NLT)

⁹ They were just trying to intimidate us, imagining that they could discourage us and stop the work. So I continued the work with even greater determination

¹¹But I replied, "Should someone in my position run from danger? Should someone in my position enter the Temple to save his life? No, I won't do it!"

Prayer

God You never cease to astonish me. Your goodness and mercy is priceless. God, I thank You for keeping me and many others through the raging storms these last few days. God, I lift those families up to You who lost their homes and even love ones. God comfort them at this time and send Your angels to not only pray but to also offer a helping hand to those in need. God keep us all and protect us. Lord for the true believers see that we are living in the last days. Nature seems to be out of balance as man becomes more and more detached from You. But God, the true Christians know what to do, how to do it and are equipped to do it according to Your word. God, I ask that You strategically place Your people in the areas and places where needed. Guide our footsteps and our tongues. God we will speak Your peace, grace, mercy, and perfect order in these places. God we acknowledge Your power over all that will be spoken, thought, decided, and done within these walls. Energize us when we grow tired, and let us continue to be the light that we are assigned to be. Thank You for opportunity to serve You, and for ALL that You have done, everything that You are doing, and everything You are going to do. Amen!!! *Flowing From Sarita's Heart & Pen.*

GOD IS UP TO SOMETHING GREAT!!!

INSPIRED THOUGHTS . . .

There is a shifting in the spiritual realm. Can you feel it? Open your eyes as well as your heart. Has some things happened in your life that you really can't explain or understand? No, it's not a mistake; it is God doing what He does. Accept His will and keep it moving my sisters and brothers!!!—*From Sarita's Pen*

SCRIPTURE

Psalm 35:27 (KJV)

27Let them shout for joy, and be glad, that favor my righteous cause: yea, let them say continually, Let the LORD be magnified, which hath pleasure in the prosperity of his servant.

Psalm 77:13 (NLT)

13 O God, your ways are holy. Is there any god as mighty as you?

Psalm 96:4 (NLT)

4 Great is the Lord! He is most worthy of praise! He is to be feared above all gods.

PRAYER

God thank You for Your faithfulness and Your brand new mercies I see daily. There are no words that can explain Your goodness. I am in awe of Your greatness and how You have blessed Your people even when it does not appear that way to man. I only ask one thing of You today God and that is bless all that faithful to reading Your word daily. I pray that the scripture and thoughts change hearts and minds as we watch You work in our lives, and see Your greatness. Amen!!! ***Flowing From Sarita's Heart & Pen***

am innocent. From now on I will go preach to the Gentiles." [7] Then he left and went to the home of Titius Justus, a Gentile who worshiped God and lived next door to the synagogue

PRAYER

Today God, I come before Your throne of grace thanking You for stepping in and reconstructing my life. Sometimes we don't understand Your ways, but from experience I can say, I no longer ask questions for I believe Jeremiah 29:11 (NLT) that states "For I know the plans I have for you, declares the LORD, plans to prosper you and not to harm you, plans to give you hope and a future. God, I thank You for preparing me to walk in spiritual authority and giving me favor in every area of my life. God there were so many days I wanted to give up these last few months, but You always send a word of encouragement through my true friends and even strangers that I do not know. But I know now they were angles looking after me. God so many times things have happen in my life that I can't explain, but I know that it was You who had Your hands on me. I thank You for that!!!!!! God as I enter a new stage of my life, I know that You are doing something bigger and supernatural that will be a blessing to many. I now understand even more how and why You are preparing me in every area of my life (spiritual, relationships, knowledge/career, etc.). God bless everyone reading this word You have given me today. Bless their homes, families, and even their jobs. Where there is confusion, give them clarity. Where there is disorder, give them peace. God, I speak blessings over marriages. God, I pray that each couple will come together in prayer and cast down every stronghold in their marriages. For the enemy does not like the institution of marriage and will destroy it every chance he gets. But God You have given all Your children the power over the enemy. Luke 10:19 (NLT) states it best "Look, I have given you authority over all the power of the enemy, and you can walk among snakes and scorpions and crush them. Nothing will injure you." We must tap into that power to take back the institution of marriage; Take back our families, our children, our schools, our streets, our country and yes even some of our churches who have gone astray. God, I pray for the spirit of humility and the spirit of boldness in Christ as well. God balance is what we as Christians need. Humble enough to love and not curse our enemies, but bold enough to speak to the enemy in the name of Jesus to cast down the spirits of darkness and send them back to the pit of hell where they belong. GOD, I THANK YOU!!!!!!!!!. God bless every pastor, preacher, teacher, prophet, and apostle who proclaims Your word with boldness. Cover them from the crown of their head to sole of their feet. Give them a fresh anointing today and every day. God we as Christian's today recommit ourselves to the works of building up Your Kingdom and tearing down the kingdom of darkness by, praying, reading Your word (Bible), and applying Your word in our daily lives. Faith without works is dead. We will live a life of devotion to You, but not as a hypocrite. We can't live so holy until we are no earthly good. When we fall down, we will get back up repent, pray, not live in the past and keep it moving. We as Christians must infiltrate every area of life. Ministry goes beyond the four walls of the churches. God bless now and I proclaim declare and decree that we as Christians by the power of the Holy Spirit will move and recommit ourselves to *Your works.* It is so!!! Amen!!! ***Flowing From Sarita's Heart & Pen***

The Power of Standing and Moving

To stand for right is a risky position. But as we stand for the right, God will supply the might!!!—**From Sarita's Pen**

Scripture

Acts 23:1-5 (NLT)

[1] Gazing intently at the high council, Paul began: "Brothers, I have always lived before God with a clear conscience!" [2] Instantly Ananias the high priest commanded those close to Paul to slap him on the mouth. [3] But Paul said to him, "God will slap you, you corrupt hypocrite! What kind of judge are you to break the law yourself by ordering me struck like that?" [4] Those standing near Paul said to him, "Do you dare to insult God's high priest?" [5] "I'm sorry, brothers. I didn't realize he was the high priest," Paul replied, "for the Scriptures say, 'You must not speak evil of any of your rulers.'" (BUT PAUL STOOD)

Prayer

God this morning I thank You for strength to do what needs to be done. I pray that as this day goes on, we all remember who and whose we are and not allow people to shake our trust in You and Your power. God, I speak a spirit of perseverance today. You are the source of our strength. We must stand for something or fall for anything. For You have not given us the spirit of fear and WE WILL NOT be a coward soldier. I AM PATIENT, I AM COMPLETE, and I LACK NOTHING!!!!!! Amen!!! ***Flowing from Sarita' Heart & Pen***

GOD'S WILL AND HIS WAY . . . . BUT DO YOU REALLY WANT HIS WAY?

INSPIRED THOUGHTS . . . .

Many times we as Christians say Lord your will and your way. But do we really want his way? Sometimes God's ways are not easy. His ways takes us down paths we would not have traveled. His ways may result in challenges and the shedding of many tears. But in the end, God's ways makes us stronger, supplies our needs, sets us up for success, and prepares us for the next assignment at a higher level. I am just speaking from experience.—*From Sarita's Pen*

God gave each of us a will. He can't enhance your life if you will not allow Him. Let God be God. And one more thing, stop giving the enemy so much credit for the negative things that happen in your life. You as a Christian knew better, but it was YOU who chose to do wrong. You may be tempted, but you have control over you. You don't have to fall!!!—**From Sarita's Pen**

SCRIPTURE

Job 22:21-23 (NLT)

Submit to God, and you will have peace; then things will go well for you. ²² Listen to his instructions, and store them in your heart. ²³ If you return to the Almighty, you will be restored—so clean up your life.

PRAYER

God thank You for the many trials and tribulations I have encountered. I can truly say they are making me a much stronger, tougher, and bolder woman of God. Thank You for placing angels in my life that look out for me, love me, and give me godly advice. God, I thank You for placing me in people lives to be a blessing and a servant. For I know it's not about me, but it is about Your Kingdom expansion!!! Lord, I gladly accept the assignment of being a servant for You and serving Your people as I walk in the Kingdom Authority that is available to all Your children. God, I pray that Your servants will truly open our eyes and ears to know that You do not want them walking around powerless. This is the trick of the enemy. Satan wants to keep all in ignorance when it comes to the power that we as Christians should possess. God, I pray that every pastor would truly teach Your people about the power and authority that are available to them through the Holy Spirit. God supply all our needs according to Your riches in glory. God, I pray for those no one else is praying for. Meet them at their needs. God guide our footsteps and guide our tongues. God You are the author and the finisher of our destiny. God, I thank You for giving me what I need and not what I want. Amen!!! ***Flowing From Sarita's Heart & Pen.***

DO WHAT'S RIGHT . . . .
LIVE AND NOT DIE

INSPIRED THOUGHTS . . . .

In Acts 5, Sapphira chose to support her husband in a lie even though she knew their actions were wrong, and as a result she died as well. This is an example of pleasing the flesh instead of the Holy Spirit. In the spirit or the physical, you don't have to die because someone else has chosen to take that route. Each one of us is held accountable, and we must watch who we have an agreement with. Yes husband and wives are to be as one once they are married. Together they may stand, but each is accountable for his or her actions. In your walk with God, do not let anyone keep you from the very call of God on your life. Yes, there are tough decisions that must be made, but upholding family in their mess is just wrong. You are no better than they are if you continue to put blinders on. No, you don't judge, but there should come a time when you say enough is enough. I am choosing to *Live.—From Sarita's Pen*

Many times we cause our own problems by putting things and people before we do God. God is a jealous God, and he will not continue to tolerate disobedience. Just think of it this way, as a parent, would you continue to let your children disrespect and slap you in the face especially if you have taken care of and love them? If you are God's child, why do you think He will continue to let you do the same to him? Selah (stop and think about it)— *From Sarita's Pen*

<u>SCRIPTURE</u>

Acts 5:1-11 (NLT)

[1] But there was a certain man named Ananias who, with his wife, Sapphira, sold some property. [2] He brought part of the money to the apostles, claiming it was the full amount. With his wife's consent, he kept the rest. [3] Then Peter said, "Ananias, why have you let Satan fill your heart? You lied to the Holy Spirit, and you kept some of the money for yourself. [4] The property was yours to sell or not sell, as you wished. And after selling it, the money was also yours to give away. How could you do a thing like this? You weren't lying to us but to God!" [5] As soon as Ananias heard these words, he fell to the floor and died. Everyone who heard about it was terrified. [6] Then some young men got up, wrapped him in a sheet, and took him out and buried him.[7] About three hours later his wife came in, not knowing what had happened. [8] Peter asked her, "Was this the price you and your husband received for your land? "Yes," she replied, "that was the price." [9] And Peter said, "How could the two of you even think of conspiring to test the Spirit of the Lord like this? The young men who buried your husband are just outside the door, and they will carry you out, too." [10] Instantly, she fell to the floor and died. When the young men came in and saw that she was dead, they carried her out and buried her beside her husband. [11] Great fear gripped the entire church and everyone else who heard what had happened

<u>PRAYER</u>

God, I thank You for strength and Your grace that empowers me to stand for what is right according to Your word. God, help each of us to understand as well that humility and Your grace empowers us. God help us to open our eyes to see that we are in a spiritual warfare and it is time out for playing church. It is out of your will and even dangerous. God, I pray each of us will come to know what Kingdom expansion is really all about. To some this message may not be a feel good message, but Lord under

Your influence, I speak to what is right. You correct each of us because You love us. I pray for those no one else it praying for. Meet them at their needs. Lord direct our footsteps and guide our tongues. God for we know that we are not perfect and we will make mistakes. Romans 3:23 (NLT) reminds us that all have sinned and fallen short of Your glory. Yes, Jesus did die for our sins and when we repent, and ask for forgiveness, he will forgive us. However, all must give an account for our actions, and no scripture in the Bible gives us a license to continue on with sin and be comfortable in it. God thank You for Your word and the Holy Spirit that guides us *if* we hear, receive, and move on Your word. I declare and decree that the blinders will be removed and the word of God will be spoken, taught and preached with **boldness** and *power* like never before. It is so!! Amen ***Flowing From Sarita's Heart & Pen.***

IT TIME TO COME OUT OF RELIGIOUS IGNORANCE

INSPIRED THOUGHTS . . .

Religious traditional "ism" and ignorance are keeping God's people in bondage. When you are in religious bondage, you don't know how to fight the enemy. As we all know, we are living in the last days and it is obvious when: a murderer can kill an innocent boy and not be arrested; the government is passing same sex marriage laws; pastors and preachers of church's are closing their eyes to hypocrisy, fornication, homosexually and blatant adultery among their leadership and even to their own mess. With all this going on, we wonder why people leave churches with such bad attitudes and hurting hearts to never return. Christ must become the *center of the church* again. Preachers, pastors, and teachers must start preaching, leading and teaching according to God's truth and not their own personal truth.—*From Sarita's Pen.*

SCRIPTURE

Acts 17:30 (NLT)

"God overlooked people's ignorance about these things in earlier times, but now he commands everyone everywhere to repent of their sins and turn to him.

PRAYER

God, I thank You for Your faithfulness. Thank You for breathing into me life daily. I am humbled that You found me worthy to walk in spiritual authority and favor. For I am a witness that You don't call the qualified, but qualify the called!!!!!!!. God, I speak life into every dead situation and a word of encouragement to press on no matter what man may forecast. You are the author and finisher of our fate. God, I pray that each of us will come to truly know who we are in You. When we move to become right in and with You, it is then all other relationships will fall into place. God, I forgive all of those who have attacked and wronged me. Bless those who have come back and apologize and even bless those who have not had the heart to do so. I realize that I must truly forgive those so that I will be forgiven for my transgressions, and move forward. God, I have learned at the end of the day, it is not about me, but about what is right in Your eyes. God sometimes I find it hard to forgive my brothers and sisters because of hurt or just pride. But Your word tells us in Proverbs 16:18 that pride goes before destruction and haughtiness before a fall. God, I also pray that each of us move with speed from religion to relationship with You. Being religious can be dangerous to Your people. We become distracted with things that are not of You. God, I pray with all my heart that each of us will come to know who and whose we are. The enemy desires to keep us in ignorance so that he can continue to lead us astray with things that look holy but in reality are leading us to the pathway of hell. God, I pray as well that the pastors would preach the word so that it breaks the yoke of ignorance and empowers Your people. Time is out for the continuous feel good messages. Your people should be taught to seek knowledge, understanding and wisdom. This is the true process of equipping the saints for spiritual warfare. Jesus tells us in John 14:12 that we should perform greater works than he. But Your people can't perform these greater works if we are tired up in "religious ignorance". God open our blinded eyes and unstop death ears in the spirit. Bless today and move in a mighty way. This is my prayer. Amen!!! **Flowing From Sarita's Heart & Pen.**

CHECK YOUR BELIEF SYSTEM

INSPIRED THOUGHTS . . . .

Ask yourself this question: What do I believe in? Do I believe in myself? Do I believe God? Do I believe . . . . STOP!!!. Please be truthful with yourself. Because if you don't truly believe God, and do not believe in yourself, it is a very good chance you don't believe that any good and positive things will manifest in your life. When you believe and trust God, everything else will fall into place. What will you believe God for today?—*From Sarita's Pen*

You know it's a little distressing to see Christians today just let the enemy run all over them while they sit back, cry, and just quote scriptures like Isaiah 54:17 (NLT) with *NO* power. You have to speak Gods word with power, authority, and belief. Because if you don' believe what you say, what makes you think your enemies will believe you. Some of us have been in church all our lives and can quote almost every scripture from Genesis to Revelation in the Bible but still have no power. Another thing, stop letting people disrespect your dreams and goals. If this is what God has given you, learn how to laugh in the enemies face and say "nice try, but I'm covered". Get a backbone in the spirit and stop having a jelly back. Every chance I get, I remind the enemy of whose I am and the power God has given me through the Holy Spirit. I'm just trying to help you along the way.—**From Sarita's Pen**

SCRIPTURE

Ephesians 1:19 (NTL)

[19] I also pray that you will understand the incredible greatness of God's power for us who believe him. This is the same mighty power

PRAYER

God thank You for the spirit of perseverance and determination. Let nothing stop me from moving forward to further understanding of You and Your ways LORD. Keep me in Your loving arms. I pray that I not stray away because in Your arms God I find safety, love, peace, prosperity and power. In Your arms, the devil in hell can't touch me. In Your arms God, I find favor and unbelievable favor that man cannot comprehend. God, I pray and believe life changing events are about to take place. God, I, receive it and will hit the ground running being a blessings to others so that it will spread like wild fire from continent to continent. God, I thank You for a vision of seeing the higher ground. God, I believe in Jeremiah 29:11 (NLT) that states: "For I know the thoughts that I think toward you, says the LORD, thoughts of peace and not of evil, to give you a future and a hope." I strive to go higher in You. You are excellent in all Your ways and in the process *I am happy being me.* I am not worried about what tomorrow brings, because I know if I stay in You LORD, my tomorrow will be exceedingly above anything that I could ever think of or imagine. God, I will continue to have an optimistic spirit because that is how You made me. I know that every day is and will not be roses, but LORD, I strive always to see the good even in the thorns. I speak blessings of faith, peace, healing, and a financial breakthrough into the atmosphere. God, I pray for those no one else is praying for. God, I pray to move forward and focus on the 'new' and not the old. Life is what I make of it, and You provide me with the gifts and tools that I need. I have everything I need if I tap into it, and if I stop listening to negative people and non-believers. I cancel out every 'dream blocker'. They have no place in my life. God, I thank You for 'the new strategy. I receive it and will walk in it. It is so!!! Amen!!! ***Flowing From Sarita's Heart & Pen***

BALANCED IN THE SPIRITUAL AND THE NATURAL"

INSPIRED THOUGHTS . . . .

Sometimes we as Christians become out of balance when it comes to the spiritual and the natural world. We go overboard in rebuking and binding spirits of failure and hindrance when all we needed to do was study and prepare for that test we failed due to not knowing the material. We pray for healing from lung cancer and diabetes when all we need to do is put the cigarettes and fried chicken away, and exercise. Discipline is the key word here. We make poor decisions and want to blame the devil for everything. We give the devil too much credit. God gave each one of us a will. We are tempted by Satan, but he does not make us perform certain acts. We are tempted, but not forced! We can't be so super spiritual until we are no earthly good. Seek God in every area of your life, he will guide you and equip you for the natural as well as the spiritual. Seek out knowledge, wisdom and understanding. This is your road map to "godly" success.—*From Sarita's Pen.*

SCRIPTURE

Deuteronomy 8:18 (NLT)

[18] Remember the LORD your God. He is the one who gives you power to be successful, in order to fulfill the covenant he confirmed to your ancestors with an oath.

James 2:26 (NLT)

[26] Just as the body is dead without breath,[a] so also faith is dead without good works.

PRAYER

God, I thank You for Your faithfulness, mercy, and grace. You are my keeper. God, I pray for those no one else is praying for. God please grant their needs. You are a God of second chances. God, I pray for those who are living a lie. They are unhappy and confused. God, I pray that reality comes upon them and they make a decision to please You and not man. Give them clarity in every area of their lives. God, I pray that they accept and embrace the *Comforter* in their lives for they will never be the same. God, I pray that each will truly seek YOU, and hear when You speak. Thank for this season of restoration, prosperity, peace, and protection. Amen!!! **Flowing From Sarita's Heart & Pen**

Real or Counterfeit Christian???

In this world today, there are some many different doctrines as it relates to Christianity. The Bible teaches us that in the last days, there will be many false prophets. 1 John 4:1 tells us to test the spirit. This is why it is crucial to read, study and live Gods word. Be who you are designed to be in God. Don't be a counterfeit Christian. This reminds me of an article I once read about the US Treasury Department. The department has a special group of men whose job is to track down counterfeiters. Naturally these men or women need to know a counterfeit bill when they see it. What's odd is that they are not trained by spending hours examining counterfeit money. But they study the real thing. They become so familiar with authentic bills that they can spot a counterfeit by looking at it or often simply by feeling it. This is what God wants us to do. Instead of focusing on the characteristics of Satan, focus on the Scriptures that gives us clearly the description of a true Christian. The distinction between the two is obvious. You then will be able to spot a *Counterfeit Christian*. Soon enough God will expose those who are deceiving his people.—***From Sarita's Pen***

Scripture

1 John 4:1 (NLT)

Dear friends, do not believe everyone who claims to speak by the Spirit. You must test them to see if the spirit they have comes from God. For there are many false prophets in the world.

1 John 4:4-6 (NLT)

⁴ But you belong to God, my dear children. You have already won a victory over those people, because the Spirit who lives in you is greater than the spirit who lives in the world. ⁵ Those people belong to this world, so they speak from the world's viewpoint, and the world listens to them. ⁶ But we belong to God, and those who know God listen to us. If they do not belong to God, they do not listen to us. That is how we know if someone has the Spirit of truth or the spirit of deception

PRAYER

God, I thank You for Your Word. Thank You for being faithful. Morning by morning new mercies I see. Thank You for being a forgiving God who looks beyond faults, and see needs. God, I pray today for those no one is praying for. God meet them at their needs. God, I pray that those who are really serious about being in right relationship with You would seek knowledge, wisdom and understanding of Your word. So then they will know You in spirit and in truth. The enemy wants to keep Your people in ignorance and he uses false prophets to do just that. The enemy does not want Your children to know who they really are in Christ. He does not want Your children to realize that they have the power to defeat him in their lives. But they must embrace the power that is given to all believers of Christ. God today I pray this epidemic of ignorance will be broken. Guide and protect. God, I pray Job 22:21-22 that tells us to agree with You quickly concerning Your will for our lives so we will have peace, and only good will come our way. Amen!!! *Flowing From Sarita's Heart & Pen*

Let God Shake, Shift, and Transform You

Inspired Thoughts . . . .

In 2011, God did some shaking in my life. The first few months of 2012, God started to shift some things in my life. At the present time, God is shaping me into the person HE needs me to be. The journey has not been easy, but I thank God for the life changing *TRANSFORMATION*!!! Life as I know it will never be the same. Anyone with me on this?—**From Sarita's Pen**

Scripture

Romans 12:2 (NLT)

Don't copy the behavior and customs of this world, but let God transform you into a new person by changing the way you think. Then you will learn to know God's will for you, which is good and pleasing and perfect.

Prayer

Thank You for an awesome day of a new awakening. You never cease to amaze me God with the things You do and how You do them. You always *make it do what it do,* and I am always grateful. God, I thank You for true ministry where people's lives are truly being transformed. God, thank You for and bless the pastors and preachers who are teaching and preaching Your word straight and with power as did the Apostle Paul. Sugar coating *The Word* will not help anyone. It will hurt in the long run. We all are held accountable for our actions once we hear and know Your word. God, Your word is power and will equip us to handle <u>all</u> situations. God many do not realize the power that is within. We must learn how to tap into this power that is given by the Holy Spirit. God this is my prayer today for all too truly establish a relationship with You and seek this which will help each of us in our everyday lives to be confident in Your word, Your guidance, Your works, and yes, themselves. God, I challenge each to seek You in every area of their lives and watch You transform them into men and women who will be a force that the enemy can't handle. This I pronounce, proclaim and decree today—Amen!!! **Flowing From Sarita's Heart & Pen**

Stop Trying to Control Others: Just Worry About Controlling YOU!

Inspired Thoughts . . . .

God wants to free you from some things that are keeping you enslaved. He wants to restore what the locusts destroyed. But most importantly, he wants to move you into the area that is productive for the Kingdom as well as for you. BUT, if you don't take control of *you*, he can't do any of these things. Remember, God gave you a will. He can't step out of heaven and make you do anything. Many times in life we let selfishness, and our own agendas keep us in the negative state that we are in and then we wonder why we are still in the valley. Pay attention to detail when God is trying to do something in your life. Surrender to "His Will" and watch your entire world change for the better.—**From Sarita's Pen**

Take charge of yourself first and not others. When you start trying to manipulate or control others is when you lose control of yourself. You are setting yourself up for failure.—**From Sarita's Pen**

Scripture

Proverbs 5:23 (NLT)

He will die for lack of self-control; he will be lost because of his great foolishness

Romans 8:3, 6, 8 (NLT)

3. The law of Moses was unable to save us because of the weakness of our sinful nature. So God did what the law could not do. He sent his own Son in a body like the bodies we sinners have. And in that body God declared an end to sin's control over us by giving his Son as a sacrifice for our sins.

6 So letting your sinful nature control your mind leads to death. But letting the Spirit control your mind leads to life and peace.

8. That's why those who are still under the control of their sinful nature can never please God.

PRAYER

Lord, I thank You for this day. Thank You for times when I can reflect on the good and the bad. You blessed me to make it through the bad and celebrate all Your goodness in every area of my life. God today, I come praying for a spirit of self-control. God help me to master self first. God, each of us all have developed habits that are irritating to You. Proverbs 5:23 (NLT) tells me that each will die for lack of self-control, and will be lost because of our own great foolishness. Please help me to change that. I only want to have good habits. Psalm 141:3 also tells me to take control of what we say, O Lord, and guard our lips. God I want to do and say the right things so that I may be a blessing to You, to my family, to my friends, and everyone I meet. Please forgive me of my sins and failures. God today I commit to You, that with Your help, I will change for the better. I praise and worship You, Lord. Amen!!! **Flowing From Sarita's Heart & Pen**

PROCRASTINATION: R U GOING TO HANDLE IT OR WILL IT HANDLE YOU?

When the spirit of procrastination tries to block your window of opportunities, push, kick or do whatever you need to do to clear this area. It is necessary to fight for what the enemy is trying to steal. This is your life and only you can control you.—**From Sarita's Pen.**

SCRIPTURE

Proverbs 19:15(NLT)

Lazy people sleep soundly, but idleness leaves them hungry.

PRAYER

God today I come boldly before Your throne of grace thanking You for peace. God thank You for the many men and women of God You have placed in my life. Thank You for opening my eyes to see the bigger picture and dream again. God thank You for moving the *dream blockers* out of the way. God, I pray that each of us will start to dream again and dream even bigger. But most of all, I pray they each of us put in place an action plan to pursue our dreams. God You tell us in Jeremiah 29:11 (NLT) that you know the plans that you have for each of us. Plans that are good and not for disaster, to give us a future and a hope. So God right now we are not only hearers of your word, but doers as well. God, it is time out for procrastination. You have given us the power to influence and change the world instead of watching

it go to hell because we are fearful. God you have not given us the spirit of fear. God You deserve nothing but the best from each one of us. You have blessed each one of us too much for us to turn our back on You now. God by the authority of Jesus Christ, I pronounce, proclaim and decree that 'we will' do as Hebrew 12:1 instructs us to do and that is to lay aside every weight that slows us down. God, I thank You for loving us with unconditional love, and holding each of us accountable especially if we are very well aware of Your Word. All honor and glory belongs to You. Amen!!!
Flowing From Sarita's Heart & Pen

The Power of God's Love

When you truly experience the love of God, it brings about great change in your life. You are made whole with ALL the fullness of life and power that can _only_ come from God. God is working on the inside of us and is able to do exceptionally and abundantly above anything we could ever ask or think of. He is the all loving and all-knowing God, but most importantly, God is unconditional love. Unconditional (total, absolute and unqualified) love is _powerful_. Practicing unconditional love is not easy, but with Christ, we can do all things—**From Sarita's Pen**

With guidance from the Holy Spirit, I truly became aware of me. It was then that it became a little easier for me to forgive, understand, trust, and love others—**From Sarita's Pen.**

Scripture

Ephesians 3:19-20 (NLT)

May you experience the love of Christ, though it is too great to understand fully. Then you will be made complete with all the fullness of life and power that comes from God. Now all glory to God, who is able, through his mighty power at work within us, to accomplish infinitely more than we might ask or think

Prayer

God, I thank You for this beautiful day. I thank You for blessing me with life today and the ability to give and to pour out to whomever You place in my path. Thank You once again for a second chance. Thank You for infusing me with Your Holy Spirit to be able to love and share unconditionally even if it is not accepted or returned. God, I know that it's what You want me to do. It's not easy Lord, but with You all things are possible. I am going to be who You want me to be. I am going to go where You want me to go. Lord, I don't' have everything that I want or even need for that matter right now, but Lord I claim that it's on the way. I declare it, decree it and call it into existence. God bless our city and protect our children especially in a time where it seems that almost everyone has gone crazy and do not value life anymore. Some may be having financial issues but God we praise You anyhow. Some may not even have a job, but we praise You anyhow. Some maybe sick, but God we praise You anyhow. Some may be having family issues, but God we praise You anyhow. Whatever situation may be right now, I praise You God anyhow. In all things I give You praise. For Praise is my weapon. Praise confuses the enemy when we praise You God while we are facing adversity. God, I claim a positive difference will be made in some one's life today. As a true child of God, selfishness is not an option. God guide my footsteps and guide my tongue. Bless You LORD as I engage today in a praise party. And God for those who do not feel this prayer and are rebellious, Lord bless them anyhow. IT IS SO! Amen. **Flowing From Sarita's Heart & Pen**

The Ultimate Power Source

Because of the state of the world at the present time, many feel powerless in my areas. The economy down; jobs being lost; family losing homes, and the list goes on. You may feel powerless to do anything. Nevertheless, you have power within. You have the power of thought. This is something no man can take from you. You can think yourself happy in any situation. You may not have control over many things, but you and only you have control over you. 2 Timothy 1:7(NLT) states for God hath not given us the spirit of fear; but of power, and of love, and of a sound mind. You are what God says you are. You are not poor, but rich. You are not sick, but well; you are not down but up. You have the ultimate power that was given to you by God. The power of the mind, when lead by God can be the ultimate weapon against any negative force.—*From Sarita's Pen*

Scripture

Proverbs 18:21 (KJV)

Death and life are in the power of the tongue: and they that love it shall eat the fruit thereof.

Luke 10:19 (KJV)

Behold, I give unto you power to tread on serpents and scorpions, and over all the power of the enemy: and nothing shall by any means hurt you.

PRAYER

Thank You for an awesome day of a new awakening. You never cease to amaze me God with the things You do and how You do them. You are always faithful, and I am always grateful. God, I thank You for true ministry where people's lives are truly being transformed. God thank You for and bless the pastors and preachers who are teaching and preaching Your word straight and with power as did the Apostle Paul. Sugar coating the word will not help anyone see the truth. We all are held accountable for our actions once we hear and know Your word. God Your word is power and will equip us to handle all our situations. God many do not realize the power that is within. We must learn how to tap into this power that is given by the Holy Spirit. God this is my prayer today for all too truly establish a relationship with You and seek this which will help each in their everyday lives to be confident in Your word, Your guidance, Your works, and yes themselves. God, I challenge each to seek You in every area of their lives and watch You transform them into men and women of God who will be a force that the enemy can't handle. This I pronounce, proclaim and decree today. Amen!!! ***Flowing From Sarita' Heart & Pen***

Spiritual Boot Camp: It's Time to Grow Up

You know it's a little distressing to see Christians today just let the enemy run all over them while they sit back, cry, and just quote scriptures like Isaiah 54:17 with NO power. You have to speak Gods word with power, authority, and belief. If you don't believe what you say, what makes you think your enemies will believe you. Some of us have been in church all our lives and can quote almost every scripture from Genesis to Revelation in the Bible but still have no power. Another thing, stop letting people disrespect your dreams and goals. If this is what God has given you, learn how to laugh in the enemies face and say "nice try, but I'm covered." Get a backbone in the spirit and stop having a jelly back. Every chance I get, I remind the enemy of whose I am and the power God has given me through the Holy Spirit. I'm just trying to help you along the way.—*From Sarita's Pen*

When you are moving into certain stages in your life, you can't continue to entertain negative people especially if they are hindering you from moving in the area you know God is calling you. You must love them and then give them a special gift. That gift is called "The Gift of Goodbye". I promise you that you will be ok in every area of your life.—*From Sarita's Pen.*

Scripture

Hebrews 6:1-3 (NLT)

[1] So let us leave the simple teachings about Christ. Let us grow up as believers. Let us not start all over again with the basic

teachings. They taught us that we need to turn away from doing things that lead to death. They taught us that we must have faith in God. [2] They taught us about different kinds of baptism. They taught us about placing hands on people. They taught us that people will rise from the dead. They taught us that God will judge everyone. And they taught us that what he decides will last forever. [3] If God permits, we will go beyond those teachings and grow up.

PRAYER

God thank You for opening my eyes and ears to hear You today. You always show up in good time; In Your time. You always place things in Your perfect order and they always work out for the good of those who seek You. I thank You God for the situations and the people You have placed in my life who have contributed to the wisdom I have gained that allows me to support and serve others. God, it's really sad that many are blessed with knowledge and wisdom and are too selfish to help someone else. Helping others requires more than just talk, it requires action and giving of self and time. Thank you for helping me mature spiritually in order to stand firm and be able to handle situations that I could not have handled 3 years ago. God today I pray that each of us will take time to reflect on our life and really examine their level of maturity. God we spend so much time in the past, and it hinders our future. Today I speak life and the *spirit of progression.* God as we seek to move forward let us not in any way give power to our adversary. As children of God, we should stop living beneath the standards You have set for us. We must stop accepting just anything and consult with You. People or situations may be in our life only for a reason, season, or life time. But God, I trust You to show us the difference. Patient, kind, loving and faithful are You. Amen!!! ***Flowing From Sarita's Heart & Pen***

CHRISTIANS: STAND UP FOR YOURSELF

If you don't stand up for yourself and walk according to God's plan for your life, you will not be pleasing to God. I'm coming into the truth more daily, and I *don't* live by society's religious dogma. I live by the standards of God. If it doesn't itch, I don't scratch. If it's not funny, I don't laugh. There are many times as a true Christian that you will not fit into society's norm. You should be tired of getting and trying to fit in. Just be who God design you to be. And if some don't like it, that's not your problem. Because what others think of you is none of your business. I have finally decided to not be a prisoner of anyone else insecurities. Some may say, "Sarita your message sounds angry or harsh". Well my answer to that is I'm not angry. I'm full of love now more than ever. And because of that love, I have finally taken a stand to help others believe in and love themselves. Stop letting others determine your destiny. Walk in your spiritual authority and learn who you are and whose you are in Christ. One of the major issues in the churches today is that so call religious leaders want to keep God's people in ignorance and under their control. Yes, respect leadership, but be who God design you to be and don't let anyone keep you from God's purpose for your life. Walk in your purpose!—**From Sarita's Pen**

SCRIPTURE

1 Corinthians 4:20 (NLT)

For the Kingdom of God is not just a lot of talk; it is living by God's power

Revelation 3:21 (NLT)

Those who are victorious will sit with me on my throne, just as I was victorious and sat with my Father on his throne

PRAYER

Great is Your faithfulness God. Every morning I see evidence of Your glory, mercy and power. I thank You for being faithful even when man is not, and even when I am not faithful to You. You are 'Jehovah God'. I thank You for giving me a word to speak to Your people even when it is not always received. I will continue to believe You even when there is chaos all around. I believe and proclaim that You will breathe life into every dying situation. I believe and proclaim that You will heal bodies of cancer and restore the broken heart. I believe and proclaim that You will restore finances. I believe and proclaim that You will restore relationships. I believe and proclaim that our children are victorious and have bright futures. I believe and proclaim that You will be invited back into the school system to restore order. I believe and proclaim that this country will return to "In God We Trust". God, I speak blessings into everyone's life who reads this prayer. The time is now that a stand must be taken for something or man will fall for anything. God sometimes I get tired, *but* Your word Galatians 6:9 (NLT) keeps me going. And let us not be weary in well doing: for in due season we shall reap, if we faint not." Thank You for Your word that empowers and activates my faith. I believe You for greater peace, greater power, greater protection and greater prosperity. Not just for me, but for all of Your sons and daughters. I decree! Amen. **Flowing From Sarita's Heart and Pen**

You MUST Raze Some Things in 2013 !!!!

Don't let your past hurt, pain and disappointments transform you into a bitter and evil person whose only agenda is to destroy that joy and peace you see within others. Don't allow your heart to become like stone. Just know this, if you don't raze this hardness from your heart, God will place you in positions in which you will not have a choice. A state of brokenness is sometimes good for the soul. In this state, God will humble you, and you will be forced to look at *you.—From Sarita's Pen*

Sometimes your *should have's* in life will hinder you from fulfilling your true purpose in life. Let it go !!!—*From Sarita's Pen*

You don't have to live your life at the mercy of things and people you don't enjoy or who don't bring you joy. Especially if they are tearing you down and not building you up. It's time to 'raze' these things out of your life. It's your time for happiness—*From Sarita's Pen*

Scripture

Psalms 51:1-13 (NLT)

[1]Have mercy on me, O God, because of your unfailing love. Because of your great compassion, blot out the stain of my sins. [2]Wash me clean from my guilt. Purify me from my sin. [3]For I recognize my rebellion; it haunts me day and night. [4]Against you, and you alone, have I sinned; I have done what is evil in

your sight. You will be proved right in what you say, and your judgment against me is just. ⁵For I was born a sinner—yes, from the moment my mother conceived me. ⁶But you desire honesty from the womb, teaching me wisdom even there. ⁷Purify me from my sins, and I will be clean; wash me, and I will be whiter than snow. ⁸ Oh, give me back my joy again; you have broken me—now let me rejoice. ⁹Don't keep looking at my sins. Remove the stain of my guilt. ¹⁰**Create in me a clean heart, O God. Renew a loyal spirit within me.** ¹¹Do not banish me from your presence, and don't take your Holy Spirit from me. ¹²Restore to me the joy of your salvation, and make me willing to obey you. ¹³Then I will teach your ways to rebels, and they will return to you.

PRAYER

God today and every day is a special day. It is special because You made it and we live to see it. God thank You for storms in my life because I now see they are serving a purpose. Thank You for the prophets that have spoken on the things that shall come to pass. And yes, they are coming to pass. Thank You for being patient with me and loving me. Forgive me for my sins as I forgive those who have sinned against me. God, I see and feel a shift in the spiritual realm. God today I say a special prayer for those who are true and ready to receive and move into what You have for them. I speak clarity into their lives. I speak that each will have the courage and power to walk away and cut the folks out of their lives who are holding them back. Lord it is a hard thing to do sometimes, but LORD each of us should love You more and want to be pleasing to You and not to man. I am a witness that You God will bring new friends in our lives who are on the same page. God open doors today and make things clear for Your people who have been praying to You for a long time on the next steps to take. Today O my God, You will show up and each will know that it is You. Speak LORD! As Your servant, I am excited for all who are patient, faithful, believe, and obey You. The devil can't stop Your work. All the undercover demons

Protection: God Has You Covered

Praise Gets Me Through

Inspired Thoughts

I am learning that doubt will hinder my progress, but praise gets me through—*From Sarita's Pen*

Scripture

Mark 11:23 (KJV)

For verily I say unto you, That whosoever shall say unto this mountain, Be thou removed, and be thou cast into the sea; and shall not doubt in his heart, but shall believe that those things which he saith shall come to pass; he shall have whatsoever he saith

Prayer:

I praise You God from whom all blessings flow. I praise You for not just what You have done, but for who You are. You are the Great I AM, and the lover of my soul. The one who keeps me, provides for me, protects me, and blesses me. Thank You for a day that was not promised to me. Thank You for new blessings and mercies that I don't deserve. God, I thank You for Your Holy Spirit that keeps me; pushes me, and convicts me when I want to go into doubt mode. I pray that what You have given me is a blessing to someone else. We are all blessed to be a blessing to someone else no matter what we may have. God Your measuring guidelines are not equal to that of man. I speak a word of encouragement into every situation today knowing that You will supply every need. Amen!!! *From Sarita's Heart & Pen.*

GOD WANTS TO FREE YOU, RESTORE AND MOVE YOU FORWARD, BUT . . . .

INSPIRED THOUGHTS . . .

God wants to free you up from some things that are keeping you in bondage. He wants to restore what the locusts destroyed. But most importantly, he wants to move you into the area that is productive for the Kingdom as well as for you. *But*, if you don't take control of *'you'*, he can't do any of these things. Remember, God gave you *'a will'*. He can't step out of heaven and move you do anything. Many times in life, we let selfishness, and our own agendas keep us in the negative state that we are in and then we wonder why we are still in the valley. Pay attention to detail when God is trying to do something in your life. Surrender to *'His Will'* and watch your entire world change for the better.—
From Sarita's Pen

SCRIPTURE

Joel 2:25

"I will repay you for the years the locusts have eaten—the great locust and the young locust, the other locusts and the locust swarm—My great army that I sent among you."—

Jeremiah 29 11-13(NIRV)

"I know the plans I have for you," announces the Lord. "I want you to enjoy success. I do not plan to harm you. I will give you hope for the years to come. Then you will call out to me. You will come and pray to me. And I will listen to you. When you look for me with all your heart, you will find me.

PRAYER

God, I thank You for keeping me and protecting my home last night as I slept. God, I thank You for not only protecting me, but for infusing me with a new mind this morning. Thank You for clarity and the ability to refocus. I know it was through the Holy Spirit that You, God manifest the things to come. God as I live this life daily, I understand more and more that it is You that I put my trust in. And it is through the people You send into my life that I can only trust. God, I understand more that it is You who has my best interest at heart. Man will lie to You, but You God will never lie. I can worship You God in spirit and in truth. I proclaim Isaiah 54:17(NLT) "But no weapon that is used against You will succeed. People might bring charges against You. But You will prove that they are wrong. Those are the things I do for my servants. I make everything right for them, announces the Lord." I stand on Galatians 6:9(NLT). "Let us not become tired of doing good. At the right time we will gather a crop if we don't give up." Perseverance is my song that I am singing and praises are on my lips for Your greatness. God, I pray for each of us to overcome our issues and realize that we are nothing without You. God, I pray that each will become free in You. I pray that each person will be restored and not live in past hurt and pains. God, I pray that when You bring people into our lives, we will recognize that it is You moving and not take the person for granted. But God, most of all, I pray that each will move forward in what You want for their lives. God let us be mindful of the words that leave our lips. Once they are released they can't be taken back. Life and death are in the power of the tongue. We can restore or build up a person, or we can break them down and murder their spirit. Let us think and speak with the mind of Christ who is the ultimate *word master.* Hear this prayer LORD. Amen!!! ***Flowing From Sarita's Heart & Pen***

DOING WHAT YOU MUST DO . . . .
GOD GETS THE GLORY

God's Glory shines on all his children. Don't let past hurt and pain hold you back. You *must* keep moving. You are too close now to give up. Sometimes we get close to the final destination and we fear the unknown to the point that we subconsciously may try to sabotage the mission. That is the trick of the enemy. Don't give in. You <u>must</u> keep going. Someone else's life may be tied to your action. You are not hurting just yourself, you could be hurting many.—***From Sarita's Pen***

SCRIPTURE

Philippians 3:14

I press toward the mark for the prize of the high calling of God in Christ Jesus.

PRAYER

Today God, I pray for consistency and the spirit of determination regardless of what is going on. Sometimes God, I become weary and feel like giving up, but God, I stay connected to You. You are the source of my strength. God, I pray this prayer touches many. Bless each to overcome fear and doubt. You did not promise this life would be easy. But You did say that You would never leave or forsake Your people. God, I thank You for this. God, Your words move me through many situations. The Holy Spirit gives me the strength and the power to push on and continue to 'make it do

what do'. Thank You for the spirit of perseverance. Many don't understand the drive, but God that's ok. I pray that the spirit becomes contagious. Thank You for blessing me right now to be able to express the words and thoughts that give You glory. I know that I am nothing without You. The past is the past, and I press forward. For You have shown me my future. A future filled with peace, power, prosperity and protection. I claim right now that as I submit to You, You will continue to give me what is needed to bless others. Being selfish is not an option. Blessings, glory, dominion, and power belong to You LORD. Amen!!!
Flowing From Sarita's Heart & Pen

God's Witness Protection Program

INSPIRED THOUGHTS . . .

God is performing many miracles in some of your lives. For each one of you are a gift who was made special by God. Arise and hear God calling you out of some things and into other area for his purpose. For some, God is accelerating your comeback. Now is not the time to take on a selfish attitude or let fear suppress you. I know it's hard sometimes. You plant seeds and it seems that your harvest is not producing like it should. So you pray and it seems that God does not hear you. Maybe you need to move closer to Him. Continue to move and keep planting the seeds of good, and be a witness every chance opportunity permits. The enemy will come, but do not worry for God has a hedge around you. This is the ultimate witness protection program.—**From Sarita's Pen**

SCRIPTURE

Psalm 18:2 (NLT)

The Lord is my rock, my fortress, and my savior; my God is my rock, in whom I find protection. He is my shield, the power that saves me, and my place of safety.

Psalm 18:30 (NLT)

God's way is perfect. All the Lord's promises prove true. He is a shield for all who look to him for protection.

PRAYER

God, I thank You for Your protection. What my enemies meant for bad, You flipped the script and turned it in my favor. God, I thank You for placing me in Your witness protection program. God, I intercede for my sisters and brothers this week in the areas of their finance, faith, and family. God, I pray that each will give You what belongs to You so their finances can be blessed. For the ones that are giving according to Your word, I pray a blessing of favor on their lives. God, I also pray that each will let go of 'that' situation and let You have the situation believing that You have already worked it out. God, I pray for the families that are divided. God bring them closer together. I pray that each will have an open mind and heart to let Your love come in. God with situations being as they are at the present time, it is very easy for the enemy to come in and destroy finances, faith and the family. But God, the book of Revelation speaks of these times of trials and tribulations, but it also speaks of the victory. We have won and some have yet to realize this. We only look at 'the now' and not the future. This too shall pass. In John 16:33 (KJV), Jesus stated that he has already overcome the world. On a personal note, God, I thank You for the comeback. Thank You for restoring me to just 'be' me in You. I don't worry about what people say or do. It is no longer a concern. I am determined that nothing shall separate me from Your love. All that You have equipped me with will be used for You in helping Your people. God, I pray that I will continue to walk in my gifts and use them according to Your word. Not only will others be blessed, each will be blessed far above anything they could ever imagine. It is so! Amen!!!!
Flowing From Sarita's Heart & Pen.

Don't Waste Your Time With Unproductive People: God Has Your Back!!!!

Don't waste your time with unproductive and small minded people especially if you have done all you can. You have ministered, prayed, fast, and anointed. Now you are totally disappointed and hurt because they fail to receive what God was trying to do in their lives. Do like the Apostle Paul, shake the dust from your clothes and move on. There are others who need you and the blessings God is trying to provide.—**From Sarita's Pen**

Scripture

Acts 18:5-10 (NKJV)

5When Silas and Timothy had come from Macedonia, Paul was compelled by the Spirit, and testified to the Jews that Jesus is the Christ. 6 But when they opposed him and blasphemed, he shook his garments and said to them, "Your blood be upon your own heads; I am clean. From now on I will go to the Gentiles." 7 And he departed from there and entered the house of a certain man named Justus, one who worshiped God, whose house was next door to the synagogue. 8 Then Crispus, the ruler of the synagogue, believed on the Lord with all his household. And many of the Corinthians, hearing, believed and were baptized. 9 Now the Lord spoke to Paul in the night by a vision, "Do not be afraid, but speak, and do not keep silent; 10 for I am with you, and no one will attack you to hurt you; for I have many people in this city."

PRAYER

God today I thank You for Acts 18. God, I know from experience that everyone will not receive a word of encouragement and knowledge from You. But God, there is always others who need what You are giving. God, I speak a word of encouragement for those who are Your 'lights' in the workplace and in their families. Strengthen them and send Your angels to minister to them when they become tired and frustrated. God, I pray today a covering over everyone praying this prayer with me. God, I pray that each will keep the faith. Psalm 27:14 (NLT) tells us to "Wait patiently for the Lord. Be brave and courageous. Yes, wait patiently for the Lord." Blessings are ours and the rewards are great if we faint not. Amen!!!! **Flowing From Sarita's Pen.**

When God Reveals Things to You, Be Prepared to Accept Them and Move On"

Inspired Thoughts . . .

When God reveals things to you, be prepared to accept them and move on. It may disappoint you, but He is only looking out for you because he loves you and has your best interest at heart. He knows more than you and He will get you through. Admit how you feel. You can't deal with what you can't acknowledge. Look inside yourself and then look up to God. Focus on God's past faithfulness. Remember you don't have to understand what God is doing. For God's ways are not our ways. Jeremiah 29:11 (NLT) tells us that God knows the plans that he has for us. They are plans for good and not for disaster, to give us a future and a hope. Just because you can't figure out what God is doing right now does not mean that it will not make sense later. Romans 8:31(KJV) reminds us that if God is for us, who can be against us.—*From Sarita's Pen & Elder Vickie Johnson, Morning Inspiration (October 18, 2010)*

Scripture

Ecclesiastes 7:13-14 (NLT)

Accept the way God does things, for who can straighten what he has made crooked? Enjoy prosperity while you can, but when hard times strike, realize that both come from God. Remember that nothing is certain in this life.

Prayer

Thank You for this day God. Thank You for my being able to see, to hear, to speak, to move this morning. Forgive me this day for everything I have done, said or thought that was not pleasing to You. I'm blessed because You are a forgiving and understanding God. You have done so much for me. I have witnessed Your hand of blessing, Your miraculous power in my life and the lives of those I love. You just keep blessing me. Thank You for the gift of discernment and how YOU continue to bless me to use this gift to build up Your Kingdom. You always look out for me and protect me from the traps of the enemy. Please keep my friends, my family, my church family, and me safe from all danger and harm. God please continue to clear my mind of distractions so that I can hear from You and please direct my steps today. Thank You for Your faithfulness. ***Flowing From Sarita's Heart & Pen.***

Change, a Long Time
Coming . . . . Trust God

Inspired Thoughts . . . .

Many times we miss our blessings because we are unwilling to change. God's ways are not our ways and when He moves, he is not only thinking of just you. I believe that when God acts, that one act will result in life changing situations for many. We may not always see the blessing through the situation, but it is there. In due time, it will manifest.—*From Sarita's Pen*

Scripture

Proverbs 3:5-6 (NLT)

Trust in the Lord with all your heart; do not depend on your own understanding. Seek his will in all you do, and he will show you which path to take.

Jeremiah 29:11(NLT)

11 For I know the plans I have for you," says the Lord. "They are plans for good and not for disaster, to give you a future and a hope.

Prayer

God, I thank You for the wind of change that is in the air for Your appointed people. God from experience, I do understand that when You shake, shift and release, nothing but blessings will be produced. It may not always feel or look good, but in

You I trust. Bless every person praying this prayer with me. Bless their homes and their health. I speak a word of patience and understanding over everyone whose lives are about to be effected. God, I praise You in advance for my sisters and brothers who are about to experience Your overflow of blessings. Proverbs 3:10(NLT) tells us that You will provide not only enough, but overflow. God, I pray that when overflow is received, that each will member to be a blessing to others. You are good and Your mercy and grace are abundant. Thank You for always being here and having my back. Thank You also for the angels You send in my life. Continue to increase in me so that I will be a greater blessing to others. Amen!!! ***Flowing From Sarita's Pen.***

RESTORATION & FAVOR: DON'T LET YOUR GUARD DOWN AND STAY FOCUS

INSPIRED THOUGHTS.

Beware my sisters and brother in Christ for when you are surrounded by a bubble of favor, your enemies are always looking for the biggest pin they can find.—*From Sarita's Pen*

SCRIPTURE

Colossians 2:8 (NLT)

[8] Don't let anyone capture you with empty philosophies and high-sounding nonsense that come from human thinking and from the spiritual powers of this world, rather than from Christ.

2 Peter 3:17 (NLT)

[17] I am warning you ahead of time, dear friends. Be on guard so that you will not be carried away by the errors of these wicked people and lose your own secure footing.

PRAYER

God today I come thanking You for Your covering, Your correction, Your love, Your grace, Your mercy, Your word, Your faithfulness, and Your favor. God no words can express Your goodness. Even when the situation looks dark, You always make a way. Sometimes God, I don't always understand Your actions, but I trust You and know that You are working it out not only for my good, but for the good of all who truly love You. God, I am learning to appreciate this and just keep it real with myself and others. God sometimes I become angry at the ignorance of some people especially in the work place, but through it all, I trust You. I KNOW that You have all Your children's best interest at heart. God today I pray for the families of the victims in Arizona. I lift them up to You and pray for strength and peace in their hearts. God, I pray for the entire city of Memphis, TN as many have truly forgotten the real purpose of the government. I cast down the horrible spirit of selfishness and greed. I pray right now for our poor children who are caught up in the mess of the adults who are supposed to have their best interest at heart. God it is evident that the end times are near for Your word tells us that in the last days men will become lovers of themselves. But God Your word also tells us that You will destroy all evil doers. God, I am so glad that YOU shifted me to truly move from *religion to relationship*. Having a true relationship with You makes this journey easier for Your word and Your peace keeps me grounded. God, I am more concern with Your revelation than my reputation. Bless every person praying this prayer with me today in a mighty way. Cover, correct, and protect each of us as we move from religion to relationship with You. Amen!!! ***Flowing From Sarita's Heart & Pen.***

A Call to Witness: Another Day . . . . Another Chance

Inspired Thoughts . . .

Today is a good day to start freeing your life of toxicants. These toxicants could be a bad habit, bad attitude, or a person (people). Going through a *spiritual detoxification* does not feel or look good. The purpose of the process is to purge your system of things that can harm you, or could even one day kill you. But in the end, you can be who God wants you to be and start living a life that is your own. Moving *'into'* God helps build your faith and staying power. As a Christians, there is one thing we must be cautious of and that is repeating negative cycles. If you see the results of the same repeated behavior is harmful, why would you continue on this path? Is it because it's comfortable? Get out your comfort zone because your comfort zone is one that is causing you nothing but hurt, pain, and regret. This same repeated behavior is not only draining you, but the people around you. Shift your thought process. Love differently, live life differently, and let God. For once in your life step out, step up, and get it right.—***From Sarita's Pen***

Women of God will you just stop it! As women, we are creatures with the continued thought process of "I got to do this or I have to do that now!!!" Yes, please be about your business, but sometimes we don't hear God when He tells us "I got this". Beware in all of your busyness. One day God may send that blessing you have been praying for to your address and you are on the other side of town at an address that was not on God's list for you to visit.—***From Sarita's Pen Scripture***

2 Chronicles 20:17 (NLT)

But you will not even need to fight. Take your positions; then stand still and watch the Lord's victory. He is with you, O people of Judah and Jerusalem. Do not be afraid or discouraged. Go out against them tomorrow, for the Lord is with you!"

Romans 8:31(KJV)

What shall we then say to these things? If God be for us, who can be against us?

Prayer

God, I thank You for new blessings I see today. Thank You for always working things out for Your people. God today, I just want to pray a prayer of thanksgiving. God, If You never do anything else for me, You have done exceedingly above anything I could ever ask or think of. Life is precious and no matter what happens or comes my way, I trust You. God, I personally thank You for Your favor and looking out for me. One job was eliminated but You created another one. Thank You! I thank You for Your favor that is manifesting in my life and LORD *I know that I know that I know that You are good and Your mercy continues forever.* Hallelujah!!! For great is Your faithfulness. God, I speak life, a renewed spirit, and peace into the air today by the power of the Holy Spirit. God, I pray for my sisters and brothers who find themselves transiting in life. God, I pray strength and courage for them. I pray each will seek You in every area of their lives. For Psalm 105:4 (NLT)states "Search for the Lord and for his strength; continually seek him." Matthew 6:33 (NLT)states "Seek the Kingdom of God above all else, and live righteously, and he will give you everything you need." I pray that when You speak, Your people will hear Your voice today. I cast down every form of distraction that attempts to throw them off the path of their designed destiny. God, I thank You for trusting and using me to be a witness for You. A form of witnessing that impact lives with a real perspective on life and living life well in Christ. Amen!!! *Flowing From Sarita's Heart & Pen.*

Halter, Hater, or Healer: Which R U?

Inspired Thoughts . . . .

If you want your problems resolved, pray and intercede for others while you are going through your own storm. You can't always get caught up in your own issues. God will work them out for you IF you let him. He needs you to walk in your purpose and help your sisters and brothers. You must live for a cause greater than yourself IF you want to be an effective Christian. As I surrendered to Him, I thank God for teaching me this principle.—*From Sarita's Pen*

Scripture

Psalm 138:7 (NLT)

Though I am surrounded by troubles, you will protect me from the anger of my enemies. You reach out your hand, and the power of your right hand saves me.

1 Corinthians 12:9 (NLT)

The same Spirit gives great faith to another, and to someone else the one Spirit gives the gift of healing.

Prayer

God, I come to You today with a troubled spirit praying for my sister(s) and brother(s) who are holding on to past hurt and pain. God, I pray each will give their hurt to You. Some have given their hurt to You before, but have picked it up again and continued to hold on to it. Let each cry out to You and admit that they are broken and need Your help. Break the prideful spirit. God, I lift those up who are still hurting from childhood pains. God, I lift those up who are still hurting from bad relationships of the past and the present. God, I lift those up who are still grieving over a love one who have passed on. God, I lift up those who are hurting overall, and feel they have nowhere else to turn. God, I cast down any signs of depression or suicidal thoughts. God, I speak against any form of demonic thoughts that maybe going through their minds right now. God right now I ask You to infuse each with the Holy Spirit . . . . The Comforter. You O God will give an inner peace that only You can give. God please just breathe on each, and reform their spirits from the inside out. God, I speak against a disobedient and rebellious spirit. God, I pray for a breakthrough and a release. God You said in Your word that You would never leave or forsake us. God right now I speak from experience, there is a brighter day. I am living it right now!!!! God You have been there for me through hell and high waters. God You have helped me deal with childhood issues; generational curses; depression, insecurities, bad relationships, verbal abuse, and yes even suicidal thoughts as a teen. God, I thank You right now!!!!! You have always been there even when the devil tried to take me out through a love one. But God, I am still here and a witness that I overcame by Your grace and mercy. God for my sisters and brothers can and will overcome. You are a God of peace, comfort and protection. God, I pray that someone will change their path today and reach out to You. Give them the kind of peace that when they are alone, they are not lonely. Give them the kind of peace that when people speak nasty and untrue things about them, they don't think twice about it for they know who they belong to. God You are awesome and I pray that each will truly come to know Your *awesomeness*. Every prayer that I prayed today God, I call it into existence. For someone will be set free. Amen!! ***Flowing "Strongly" From Sarita's Pen.***

HE SAYS I GOT YOU . . . .
KEEP MOVING!!!

<u>THOUGHTS</u> . . .

Identify your enemies so you can move on. When you know what you are dealing with, you know how to handle it. Move to the higher ground God has for you. You will then not drown in your enemy's floods of detractions—***From Sarita's Pen***

Every time you set a trap for me, it backfires and you fall into it. Why not take that same energy and set some positive examples instead of traps. You will save yourself some heartache, pain and disappointment.—**From Sarita's Pen**

<u>SCRIPTURE</u>

1 Samuel 2:9 (NLT)

He will protect his faithful ones, but the wicked will disappear in darkness. No one will succeed by strength alone

<u>PRAYER</u>

"But in that coming day no weapon turned against You will succeed. You will silence every voice raised up to accuse You" (Isaiah 54:17 NLT) This is Your word God that I have been standing on for a long time now, and You have never failed me. Thank You!!! Proverbs 16:7(KJV)tells us also that when people's lives please the Lord, even their enemies are at peace with them. Thank You once again. I pray that You cover everyone praying this prayer with me. Bless each to receive Your word and stand

firm on Your word. God I will position Myself to stand still and watch You work my enemies so that what was intended for evil will turn out for my good and You receive the glory. Amen!!!!!
Flowing From Sarita's Heart & Pen

BE NOT WEARY. KEEP FIGHTING!!!

Action Required:

- Stand still—(stop moving and shut up!!!!)
- Pray—(Have a conversation with God)
- Press—(Press into God)
- Listen (Listen to God and not yourself or outside noise)
- Move—(Be ready to move when God speaks)

—*From Sarita's Pen*

Stand still and watch God work when your enemies try to destroy your self-esteem. Remember keep reading the word of God, praying and praising. Move with authority when God gives you instructions. Promotion comes not from man *but God!!!* As you stand boldly as a child of the King, you need to tell your enemies this: *'Back up off me. You have messed with the wrong Christian today!!!'*—*From Sarita's Pen*

SCRIPTURE

Galatians 6:9 (KJV)

9And let us not be weary in well doing: for in due season we shall reap, if we faint not

PRAYER

Exalted are You LORD and awesome is Your name!!! Thank You for Your mercy, grace and Your favor. This is the season of uninterrupted manifestations for those who are seeking and worshiping You. God today, I intercede for those who are struggling with patience. God, I pray that the situations some may be going through will teach them patience. Psalm 37:34 tells us to wait on You Lord, and keep Your ways. You Lord will exalt us to inherit the land, and we will see the corrupted destroyed. God, I claim it right now. God show favor to those who desire a closer relationship with YOU, and who are seeking to live and do right according to Your word. We belong to and serve an awesome King, therefore, we are royalty. God, I speak blessings over everyone praying this prayer with me. I pray that each person receive this and get this deep down in their spirit that "I am *The Kings Kid*. Amen, Amen, Amen!!! ***Flowing From Sarita' Heart & Pen.***

LOVE & PROTECTION: SPEND SOME TIME WITH HIM FOR HE HAS YOUR BACK

INSPIRED THOUGHTS . . .

Do you really have time for God in your life? Be honest with yourself. We 'church' on Sundays hoping to get God out the way to say 'I have given God his time'. We don't pick up the bible until the following Sunday. And when we are asked by the preacher to find a certain passage of scripture in the Bible, we must to go the table of content every time and then figure out if it is in the old or new testament and . . . . well enough of that. That's a different topic within itself. We don't put in the time with God, yet when a negative situation happens in our life, we want God to stop what he is doing and fix our situation. Do you ever think about what would happen if God, Ignored you like you did him? It would not be pretty. But because God is a merciful and a loving God, he steps in right on time in spite of our mess. But stop and really think about it. If you were proactive instead of reactive in spending time with God, maybe some of the issues in your life would not find you, because God would intercept them before they got to you. That is called the protection and favor of God. Psalm 31:19 & 23 (NLT) states: "How great is the goodness You have stored up for those who fear You. You lavish it on those who come to You for protection, blessing them before the watching world. Love the Lord, all You godly ones! For the Lord protects those who are loyal to him, but he harshly punishes the arrogant." Seek God not just for the fact of wanting something from him. Seek him because it is the right thing to do. When you put God first in your life, you will live a life of peace, power, protection and yes prosperity. *Selah* (stop and think about it). **From Sarita's Pen**

God is performing many miracles in some of your lives. For each one of you are a gift who was made special by God. Arise and hear God calling you out of some things and into his purpose for you. For some, God is accelerating your comeback. Now is not the time to take on a selfish attitude or let fear suppress you. I know it's hard sometimes. You plant seeds and it seems that your harvest is not producing like it should. So you pray and it seems that God does not hear you. Maybe you need to move closer to Him. Continue to move and keep planting the seeds of "good" and being a witness every chance opportunity permits. The enemy will come, but do not worry for God has a hedge around you. This is the ultimate witness protection program.—*From Sarita's Pen*

SCRIPTURE

1 John 4:7-12 (NLT)

Dear friends, let us continue to love one another, for love comes from God. Anyone who loves is a child of God and knows God. [8] But anyone who does not love does not know God, for God is love. [9] God showed how much he loved us by sending his one and only Son into the world so that we might have eternal life through him. [10] This is real love—not that we loved God, but that he loved us and sent his Son as a sacrifice to take away our sins. [11] Dear friends, since God loved us that much, we surely ought to love each other. [12] No one has ever seen God. But if we love each other, God lives in us, and his love is brought to full expression in us.

Numbers 14:9 (NLT)

Do not rebel against the Lord, and don't be afraid of the people of the land. They are only helpless prey to us! They have no protection, but the Lord is with us! Don't be afraid of them!"

PRAYER

God thank You for new revelation. God, I thank You for being there when no one else was there. You said in Your word that You would never leave or forsake me. God thank You for letting me know that now is not the time to do just nothing. NOW is the time God to live and not die. Now is the time to fight and not give up. Your word tells me that we fight not against flesh and blood but against spiritual wickedness in high places. I am also reminded in Your word that I can do all things through You God and You have not given me the spirit of fear, but of a sound mind. God You remind me once again that Jesus has already overcome the world. We have to just live and seek first Your Kingdom. God, I thank You for peace today, and I know that You have equipped me with all that I need. God, I thank You for placing the right people in my life who have blessed me. God, I pray to bless them even more. God, I thank You for letting me walk in my "It". God, I thank You for re-establishing me and I look forward to being that servant You would have me to be walking in humility and boldness at the same time. God, I pray for those no one else is praying for and ask You to move in a mighty way concerning my sisters and brothers who are still stuck and don't know what to do. The word I have for each is to 'just live' and 'listen' for You to speak to them. Life is not easy, but You God have all the answers and with You there is nothing too hard. God, I thank You for my freedom not just in the natural, but in the spirit. No weapon that is formed against this freedom that You have given me shall prosper. For the weapon is D.O.A. (dead on arrival). It is so!!! Amen! ***Flowing From Sarita's Heart & Pen***

God's Anger
Management Program

Inspired Thoughts . . .

Anger is a normal and natural emotion. However, when you let your anger consume you and dictate nearly everything you say or do, it may become an illness. If you find that you are always angry and agitated, this is the time to seek help. Cry out to God he will hear you, and he will direct your path. Those directions may sometimes include seeking medical attention. God placed doctors here on earth for a reason. A very well-known physician in the bible was Luke.—***From Sarita's Pen***

Scripture

Ephesians 4:26 (NLT)

And "don't sin by letting anger control you. "Don't let the sun go down while you are still angry

James 1:19 (NLT)

Understand this, my dear brothers and sisters: You must all be quick to listen, slow to speak, and slow to get angry.

Prayer

God, I thank You for Your guidance's and protection. Thank You for keeping Your loving arms around me and protecting me. But most of all, God, I thank You for Your peace. Philippians 4:7(NLT) tells us that we will experience Your peace, which exceeds anything we can understand. Your peace will guard our hearts and minds as each live in Christ Jesus. God fill Your people with Your divine spirit, and I pray each will be open to receive what You have for them today. God, I pray that each will sit still and watch You work things out for them. Give them a peace today they have never felt before. In Jesus name I pray. Amen! **Flowing From Sarita's Heart & Pen**

Don't Get Stuck In _____.

God has better things for you to do than get stuck in the middle of disarray. That is exactly what the enemy wants to keep you enslaved to chaos and confusion!!! People will lie on you and tell all kinds of untruths. These actions are to keep you from walking into the *greatness* that God has for you. But I tell you, let it go and let God handle the situation. Romans 12:19 (NLT) says it best: "Dear friends, never take revenge. Leave that to the righteous anger of God. For the Scriptures say, I will take revenge; I will pay them back, says the Lord." Just tell yourself, God will deal with this, cover and prosper me at the same time. He is 'awesome' like that.—**From Sarita's Pen**

Identify your enemies so you can move on. When you know what you are dealing with, you know how to handle it. Move to the higher ground God has for you. You will then not drown in your enemy's flood of distractions—**From Sarita's Pen**

Scripture

Psalm 138:7-8 (NLT)

[7] Though I am surrounded by troubles, you will protect me from the anger of my enemies. You reach out your hand, and the power of your right hand saves me. [8] The Lord will work out his plans for my life—for your faithful love, O Lord, endures forever. Don't abandon me, for you made me.

PRAYER

God, I thank You for the spirit of perseverance. I thank You for the spirit of determination to press forward into my destiny and not look back. God, I see myself in the future. God, I pray this spirit upon everyone praying this prayer with me. God, we can do all things through You if we believe and know that we are free in You. You can handle every problem and every situation we have. God, I speak greater peace in the air. I speak life into everyone's situation. God let them not be ashamed of their past. For You, O God are their present help and their future. God, the enemy has so many people fooled and enslaved to his ways. But God, I pray with power and authority over my brothers and sisters that each will not listen to the enemy and that chains are falling off now as this prayer is being prayed. God, I thank You for freedom!!!! I thank You for inner peace. I pray that all will catch this and realize that we are free and have the power over the enemy. I rebuke every demon on assignment that is forming weapons against Your people and ministries. I speak death to their words, plots and actions. The devil is defeated and You child of God will prosper and LIVE !!!!!! I declare it, decree it and call it done!!!! Amen!!! **Flowing From Sarita's Heart &Pen**

STAY ON COURSE AND LET GOD HANDLE THE WOLVES

INSPIRED THOUGHTS . . . .

No matter how difficult it seems, you must finish your assignment. Let God handle *the wolves* in your life. Don't try to fight them for God is your Shepherd as Psalm 23 states. You may see 'these wolves' on every side, and it may not be comfortable. But you *must* maintain your focus and keep moving and pressing on. They may growl and snap at you, but you can be assured God will protect you.—***From Sarita's Pen***

Stop pouring yourself into things and people that can't handle you. Don't be wasted—***From Sarita's Pen***

SCRIPTURE

Psalm 23 (KJV)

¹The LORD is my shepherd; I shall not want. ²He maketh me to lie down in green pastures: he leadeth me beside the still waters. ³He restoreth my soul: he leadeth me in the paths of righteousness for his name's sake. Yea, though I walk through the valley of the shadow of death, I will fear no evil: for thou art with me; thy rod and thy staff they comfort me. Thou preparest a table before me in the presence of mine enemies: thou anointest my head with oil; my cup runneth over. Surely goodness and mercy shall follow me all the days of my life: and I will dwell in the house of the LORD forever.

Romans 12:19 (KJV)

Dearly beloved, avenge not yourselves, but rather give place unto wrath: for it is written, Vengeance is mine; I will repay, saith the Lord.

Isaiah 59:18 (KJV)

According to their deeds, accordingly he will repay, fury to his adversaries, recompense to his enemies; to the islands he will repay recompense.

PRAYER

God, I thank You for visions. Thank You for great leaders who follow through on the vision You have given them. In Habakkuk 2:2 (NLT), You tell us to write the vision, and make it plain. Your word is true, and I believe and receive the promises You made to Your people. I pray for each to tap into the gifts You have given. LORD I pray that each will receive soon what their instructions are for their lives and move accordantly. There are greater things to come and time is at hand. God, I pray protection and rebuke the enemy for he will try to block and hinder the progress. But God, he has no power over Your plans. I declare it, decree it. It shall come to pass. It is so! Amen. ***From Sarita's Heart and Pen***

Prosperity: God Wants to Bless You

GOD TAKES CARE OF HIS PEOPLE. ARE YOU HIS?

Never be a prisoner of others insecurities. And never make someone a priority while they make you an option. If you are not careful, insecure people will exhaust you and take what God has placed in you to be a blessing for those who truly need it.—**From Sarita's Pen**

SCRIPTURE

Philippians 4:19 (KJV)

But my God shall supply all your need according to his riches in glory by Christ Jesus.

Ecclesiastes 2:26 (NLT)

God gives wisdom, knowledge, and joy to those who please him. But if a sinner becomes wealthy, God takes the wealth away and gives it to those who please him. This, too, is meaningless—like chasing the wind.

PRAYER

In everything I do God, I try very hard to acknowledge that You are the source of my strength. Even when I give and nothing is given in return, I still have a giving heart. This is not because of me, it is because of You. Thank You for moving and restoring what the locusts have destroyed. Thank You for unconditional love and for making me in Your image. God bless every person praying this prayer with me. I pray that each truly come to know who they are and realize who they belong to. Insecurity and fear are the enemies to Your people that also places them in a state of confusion. God, I speak against confusion and declare peace and a state of confidence. Confidence comes from seeing, believing and experiencing Your manifestation. Thank You for watching over and taking care of all my needs. The path ahead has many turns and curves, but I see Your light that will guide me to the destination You have for me. I will never apologize for my optimistic view. For You made me this way God. Victory is mine as the book of Revelations has proclaimed and with that I say Amen!!! ***Flowing From Sarita's Heart & Pen.***

Transformational Thinking: Speak Your Future and Act on It

Whatever you think you are, you are. Whatever you say you will be, you shall become, and whatever actions you take will really show who you really are.—*From Sarita's Pen*

Scripture

Romans 12:2 (NLT)

Don't copy the behavior and customs of this world, but let God transform you into a new person by changing the way you think. Then you will learn to know God's will for you, which is good and pleasing and perfect.

Proverbs 18:21 (NLT)

The tongue can bring death or life; those who love to talk will reap the consequences.

Prayer

God all praises belong to You. You are always worthy of the glory and honor. God, I come today to intercede for my sisters and brothers in Christ. God, I thank You for blessing, changing, transforming, correcting and performing miracles. God, I speak a word of healing and power over each person and their situations. God bless even more the ones who have been obedient to Your word and Your will. For they shall see Your manifestation take place in their lives. God for all who are still struggling, I pray that each will truly get in tune with You and watch Your blessings flow. God, You are just waiting to blow their minds. Thank You God for Your 'change agents' You bring into my life and for making me a change agent to bless others. God, I am a living witness that if You speak the truth, You will be blessed. God, I pray for my enemies and I ask You to handle them. I have learned that You can handle them better than I can. God, I cast down all fear and doubt for Satan does not want me to know the power I have as a Christian. But God, today I speak a word of power and authority into the air. Every time Satan tries to form a weapon against Your children, he is defeated before he starts. Thank You for transformational thinking and I pray that this prayer is will transform someone's life. God, You are always looking out for me and handle all obstacles in my path. So Satan, You have no power or authority. For all the demons on assignment, you are on your way to hell where you belong. It is so!!! Amen!!! ***Flowing From Sarita's Heart & Pen***

THANK YOU GOD FOR PREPARATION !!!

From experience, I have learned that God allows you to go through situations at an early age to prepare you for bigger situations at a later time. In essences, God is always preparing you, but not always how you may think—**From Sarita's Pen.**

SCRIPTURE

Jeremiah 29:11(NLT)

For I know the plans I have for you," says the Lord. "They are plans for good and not for disaster, to give you a future and a hope.

PRAYER

God, You always look out for Your children and I thank You. Thank You for favor, peace, power, and protection. I thank You God for this day that was not promised to me. God, I pray for each praying this prayer with me right now. Bless them. I pray for peace and understanding for each person. God, I know from experience that You prepare Your children for what is to come. I want to say thanks you!!! God, I speak a spirit of understanding and patience into everyone's lives. You have the master plan, and it is already worked out. All we have to do Father is listen and move when You say move. Right now some may not understand what is happening, but You know God. God, I thank You for the spirit of discernment, and I will continue to use this gift to bless others as You give instructions. Thank You for preparing me and showing me why You do what You do. I say Hallelujah !!!! It may not always be easy or feel good, but it always works out for my good. You God have my best interest at heart. In love I pray. Amen!!! **From Sarita's Heart & Pen**

A Test: Can I Handle the Blessing?

Inspired Thoughts . . .

Many times in life, you are put through a series of test. Sometimes you pass and sometimes you fail. You finally get what you have been praying for, but you don't know how to handle the blessing. That's why you should be careful what you pray for, and when you pray for it, make sure you can handle it. Yes, God is a god of second chances, but it is up to him if he desires to grant you that second chance. For God's ways are not our ways. So the question you should ask yourself today is "Am I "truly" ready for what I am asking for?"—**From Sarita's Pen**

Scripture

Proverbs 3:5-6

"Trust in the Lord with all your heart and lean not on your own understanding; in all your ways acknowledge Him, and He will make your paths straight."

Prayer

Many times God we pray to You for something, and we are not really ready for what we pray for. God what I have learned is that if I am faithful over a few things, You will grant me the desires of my heart. And for that I thank You. God today I pray that each will examine their hearts. God it is easy for us to make assumptions about the path we are on. God enlightened our reasoning so that we will not make the wrong choices. God sometimes our choices seem right at the time, but later we discover these choices have led us away from You because they were based on our own reasoning. I acknowledge You in all my ways today. And I am leaning completely on You to reveal Your direction for my life. If You do so, I know I will be directed to the desired destination You have for me. Amen! **Flowing From Sarita's Pen and Heart.**

Favor of God in 2011: The Desires of Your Heart

Inspired Thoughts . . .

In the Holy Bible, Galatians 6:9 reminds us to not give up in doing well for when the time is right, we will reap a reward for our faithfulness to God. The time maybe sooner than you imagine. I am determined that 2011 is truly the year of 'restoration and favor' for those who have not only been faithful, but a blessing to others. Now, how these things will come to pass may not be exactly how you think, but just remember God ways are not our ways. I will also caution you to not let yourself get side track by Satan and all his tricks. He knows what flavor you like (your weakness) and he will try to use that to cause you to miss your blessings. But you are equipped and know how to put him in his place back to hell where he belongs.—*From Sarita's Pen*

Scripture

Psalm 37:4 (NLT)

Take delight in the Lord, and he will give you your heart's desires.

Galatians 6:9 (NLT)

So let's not get tired of doing what is good. At just the right time we will reap a harvest of blessing if we don't give up.

PRAYER

My God, my friend, and my savior, I am so thankful for having a relationship with You. I thank You for moving me from religion to relationship to just be who You designed me to be even with my flaws. God, I think about David who was a man after Your heart who messed up sometimes, but You still loved him and blessed him beyond belief. God, I bless You today. I thank You for showing me Your grace and mercy and not giving me what I deserve. Thank You God for Your revelations not only for my life, but for others. Lord I speak a covering and blessings into each praying this prayer with me. Lord I pray that we will stay focus and continue to move into the things that have been spoken into and over our lives. God this is a year of action and the time has come to move so that we will not miss our blessings. Jesus told us in the Bible that we will have greater works to do after he was gone so God, so we put the cross on our shoulder and move forward to do just that. God, I cast down every distraction and ever demon on assignment that will try to block Your people's path. But God, to some You have already taken care of these obstacles and the path is clear. Thank You GOD!!! God, I pray for those no one else is praying for. Meet them at their needs. God by the power of the Holy Spirit, I speak peace into the air and rebuke the spirit of confusion. I pronounce, proclaim, and decree that success belongs to us Your people in this year of 2011. And no matter how the devil tries to stop it, he is already defeated. So go back and take Your place in the pit of hell where You belong Satan. God, I speak a word of divine revelation, and I decree for those who do not understand the power that You have given them will come to know and embrace it soon. Amen!!! ***Flowing "Strongly" From Sarita's Pen.***

THIS IS YOUR YEAR. STOP LOOKING BACK!!!

THOUGHTS

Do not live in the past, but look forward to the future. As I travel down this path, my way becomes brighter and brighter. God is the source of this light through miracles he performs, the people he places in my life, and the favor he shows me in every area of my life. Therefore, I must never forget to be 'a light' to others as well. You never know who is watching you. You may have a secret mentee and never be aware of it.—*From Sarita's Pen*

SCRIPTURES

Philippians 3:14 (NLT)

[14] I press on to reach the end of the race and receive the heavenly prize for which God, through Christ Jesus, is calling us.

1 Timothy 6:11 (NLT)

[Paul's Final Instructions] But you, Timothy, are a man of God; so run from all these evil things. Pursue righteousness and a godly life, along with faith, love, perseverance, and gentleness.

PRAYER

God, there are no words that can express Your goodness, mercy, and faithfulness. But most of all, no words can express the love You show me. I know that You love me, because it always shows even when You are correcting me. That is why I always strive to give everything that I have to be pleasing to You, and attempt to always operate and work in a spirit of excellence. Thank You for just being Jehovah God; the eternal self-existence one who keeps his covenant promises to his covenant people. Thank You also for the people that You place in my life. God, I also thank You for planting me in others' lives to be a blessing if only for a season. God, I pray for those no one else is praying for. God, I pray for Your children who suffer from low self-esteem. God give them peace and show them who they are in You. God, I pray that they come to know who they are in You <u>and</u> understand Your power. Ephesians 1:19-20 (NLT) states it even better: "I also pray that You will understand the incredible greatness of God's power for us who believe him. This is the same mighty power that raised Christ from the dead and seated him in the place of honor at God's right hand in the heavenly realms." God today nothing will happen that You and I can't handle. Your word reminds us to keep pushing on to reach the end of this race and we will be rewarded. I pray that we will open up our hearts and minds to receive Your word and the vessel chosen to pour out the word. God this is the year of walking in favor and spiritual authority. I pronounce, declare and decree that we as Your people will take back what Satan has stolen from us for many years. We will reclaim our lives and destroy every weapon that is formed not only against us, but against The Kingdom of God overall. We will eliminate the people in our lives that do not have our best interest at heart and who try to extract the very life out of us with their ungodly thinking and negative attitudes. We will stop looking back and press on with perseverance for we are determine that we will let nothing keep us from achieving greatness in every area of our lives from family, finances, career, and most importantly our relationship with You God. By the power of the Holy Spirit, I declare that it is so!!! Amen!!! ***Flowing Strongly From Sarita's Heart & Pen.***

A New Thing: Can You Get Excited About That!!!

Inspired Thoughts . . .

Seek the new and let the old be what it is *old*. If you keep going back to the old and you know it not good for you that is like going back and looking in the garbage to retrieve one week old food and re-warming it for consumption. It stinks and more than likely is toxic. It could even cause death. Choose to live and move forward to *the fresh* and *the new.*—**From Sarita's Pen.**

Scripture

Isaiah 43:18-19 (NLT)

But forget all that—it is nothing compared to what I am going to do. [19] For I am about to do something new. See, I have already begun! Do you not see it? I will make a pathway through the wilderness. I will create rivers in the dry wasteland.

Prayer

God, You are awesome in all Your ways. Thank You for each praying this prayer with me. God bless them far above anything they could ever think of or imagine. God, I pray for those no one else is praying for. Meet them at their needs. God, I pray for peace in the time of confusion. God, I pray for clarity in time of indecisiveness. God, I pray for President Obama who is being attacked on every side. Cover him from the crown of his head to the sole of his feet. Give him a fresh anointing to run this county according to Your will. In the end, YOU will get the

glory God. God, I pray for restoration in homes and in the body of Christ. So many Christians have been hurt by *church folks*. God heal them and give them the strength to push forward in Kingdom building. As Your word says, this too shall pass. God You are doing a new thing in this time and we as Christians whose ears are open and hear are waiting and watching for the manifestations that are to come even with the economy being in chaos and when it seems that people have lost their minds. Thank You for Your faithfulness. You are better to us than we are to ourselves. You always have our back and come through every time and in Your time. In everything we give thanks. The devil is defeated, and You are still LORD who will forever reign. Amen!!!
Flowing From Sarita's Heart & Pen.

Just Don't Quit: Be Patient

Inspired Thoughts . . . .

Harvest time is near. Whatever seeds you sowed are about to manifest. The question we must ask ourselves and truly think about is "What kind of seeds have I sown?" Did I sow seeds of joy, peace, happiness, love, self-control, faithfulness, patience, gentleness, and goodness? <u>OR</u> Did I sow seeds of gossip, confusion, hate, selfishness, backbiting, division, destruction, lies, unfaithfulness, unforgivness, and the sin of omission (did nothing/ignored). The Message Bible makes it very clear in Galatians 6:7-9. "Don't be misled: No one makes a fool of God. What a person plants, he will harvest. The person who plants selfishness, ignoring the needs of others—ignoring God!—harvests a crop of weeds. All he'll have to show for his life is weeds! But the one who plants in response to God, letting God's Spirit do the growth work in him, harvests a crop of real life, eternal life. So let's not allow ourselves to get fatigued doing good. At the right time we will harvest a good crop if we don't give up, or quit. Right now, therefore, every time we have the chance, let us work for the benefit of all, starting with the people closest to us in the community of faith." Now after hearing God's word, ask yourself "What can I expect?" Selah (Stop and think about it)—*From Sarita's Pen.*

Scripture

Galatians 6:9 (NLT)

So let's not get tired of doing what is good. At just the right time we will reap a harvest of blessing if we don't give up.

Romans 8:28(NLT)

²⁸ And we know that God causes everything to work together for the good of those who love God and are called according to his purpose for them.

PRAYER

Today God, I come before Your throne of grace thanking You for stepping in and reconstructing my life. Sometimes we don't understand Your ways, but from experience I can say, I don't ask questions for I believe Jeremiah 29:11 (NLT) that states "For I know the plans I have for You, declares the LORD, plans to prosper You and not to harm You, plans to give You hope and a future. God, I thank You for preparing me to walk in spiritual authority and giving me favor in every area of my life. God there were so many days I wanted to give up these last few months, but You always send a word of encouragement through my true friends and even strangers. But I know now they were angles looking after me. God so many times things have happen in my life that I can't explain, but I know that it was You who had Your hands on me. I thank You for that!!! God as I enter a new stage of my life, I know that You are doing something bigger and supernatural that will be a blessing to many. I now understand even more how and why You are preparing me in every area of my life (spiritual, relationships, knowledge/career, etc.). God bless everyone praying this prayer with me today. Bless their homes, families, and even their jobs. Where there is confusion, give them clarity. Where there is disorder, give them peace. Luke 10:19(NLT) states: "Look, I have given You authority over all the power of the enemy, and You can walk among snakes and scorpions and crush them. Nothing will injure You." God, I thank you for Your word of reassurance!!!. God bless every pastor, preacher, teacher, prophet, and apostle who proclaims Your word with boldness. Cover them from the crown of their head to sole of their feet. Give them a fresh anointing today and every day. God we as Christian's today recommit ourselves to the works of building up Your Kingdom and tearing down the kingdom of darkness by, praying, reading Your word (Bible), and applying Your word in our daily lives. Hebrew 4:2 reminds us that we must mix the Word of God with faith in order for it to profit us. We will live a life of devotion to You, but not as a hypocrite being so holy until we are no earthly good. When we fall down, we will get back up and keep it moving. We as Christians must infiltrate every area of life. Ministry goes beyond the four walls of the churches. God bless now and I proclaim declare and decree that we as Christians by the power of the Holy Spirit will move and recommit ourselves to your works. It is so!!! Amen!!! ***Flowing From Sarita's Heart & Pen***

*Random Quotes
and Prayers "From
Sarita's Pen"*

FIGHT FOR WHAT IS RIGHT

Don't give up or give in. That is exactly what the devil wants you to do. I've learned that when I am being attacked and *I know that I know that I know* that I am in Gods will. It is just the prince of darkness tempting me to sabotage the blessings that God has coming my way. You must gear up and be prepared to fight back, but you can't do that if you don't know what the word of God says. For those of us who work for people in high positions, we have a tendency to believe that the work place and our spiritually do not mix. But I beg the differ. You must ask God how to handle certain situations and make the right decisions whereas God gets that glory and not you or your boss. Strategy is one of the key words in corporate America. If you want a strategy that is sure to work, ask God, he never fails. Thinking outside the box is what he specialize in because you can't keep God in a box. So with that said you must have that fight within you and know that you are not alone.—**From Sarita's Pen**

PLANTING THE SEEDS OF PEACE WITH POWER

In order to be effective in planting the seeds of peace, you must have peace within. We express peace with an action and in most cases through words. Words are powerful and words used to express peace can be simple but have power behind it. In Mark 4:39 Jesus said three simple words "peace be still" and the wind ceased. The words Jesus spoke were not that profound, but it was the power that was behind the words. He has given you *the* same power. Use this power to bring peace in your work place, your relationships and in every area of your life. You change the world by starting with yourself first. *From Sarita's Pen*

PRAISE HIM IN ADVERSITY—MY PRAISE IS MY WEAPON

Adversity is defined as an adverse fortune or fate; a condition marked by misfortune, calamity, or distress. So how do you handle your adversity? My answer to this is by giving <u>adversity</u> *'adversity'*. Cause your adversity misfortune calamity or distress. Fight back!!!! Praise, prayer, and worship are your weapons. Through this process your adversity can turn into favor, fortune, and prosperity—***From Sarita's Pen***

PROTECTION: SELAH (STOP AND THINK ABOUT IT)

When you ask God to protect you, you need to specifically ask him to protect your mind. In the mind is where the battles start and take place"—***From Sarita's Pen.***

When your enemy digs ditches for you, don't worry. You are protected by God. Just pray, stand still, and listen for the big thump. That is the sound of your enemy falling in the ditch he put all his energy in digging for you. **From Sarita's Pen**

God protects his children in many ways mentally as well as physically. He will give you a new sense of joy and love. Don't give up, and stay connected to Him.—***From Sarita's Pen***

PEACE: SELAH (STOP AND THINK ABOUT IT)

We pray for peace, but the peace starts within us. You must have peace within yourself in order for peace to enter into your relationships with other people—**From Sarita's Pen.**

POWER: SELAH (STOP AND THINK ABOUT IT)

What are you doing with the power that God has given you? It is as simple as you either use it or lose it. God has the option of giving it to someone else who is willing to use it to do His will—***From Sarita's Pen***

If you want to see the true power of God, just watch nature—
From Sarita's Pen

Because of the state of the world at the present time, many feel powerless in my areas. The economy down, jobs being lost, family losing homes, and the list goes on. You may feel powerless to do anything. Nevertheless, you have power within. You have the power of thought. This is something that no man can take from you. You can think yourself happy in any situation. You may not have control over many things, but you and only you have control over you. 2 Timothy 1:7 (KJV) states "God hath not given us the spirit of fear; but of power, and of love, and of a sound mind." You are what God says you are. You are not poor, but rich. You are not sick, but well; you are not down but up. You have the ultimate power that was given to you by God. The power of the mind, when lead by God can be the ultimate weapon against any negative force.—***From Sarita's Pen***

PROSPERITY: SELAH (STOP AND THINK ABOUT IT)

Prosperity comes with a price tag. You must be willing to give—
From Sarita's Pen

MISTAKES HAPPEN

One thing I leaned in life is that you will make mistakes. But don't make excuses. Admit that you've made a mistake. Learn from the mistake, and then move on.—***From Sarita's Pen***

DON'T GIVE UP. RECONNECT!!!

We all have experienced the spirit of hopelessness when we are going through our trials. It is then that you must check your spiritual connection cord to God to make sure that is fully plugged in and not totally unplugged. For your best life, stay focused and stay connected to your source. God is there when man lets you down—***From Sarita's Pen***

TALK TO ME. I AM LISTENING

Some find it difficult to pray. They feel that have to use special words or spiritual terms in prayer. Just think of prayer as having a conversation with God. He understands all languages, and he hears you. God wants and yearns for you to talk to him. He will answer you, but you have to remove the noise out of your life to hear him. Listening is the key to your spiritual growth.—***From Sarita's Pen***

LISTENING

God speaks to us and tells us where we should go. Many times we don't have an issue with where we are going. We have an issue with the route (how) in which God is taking us to reach the destination. Therefore, sometimes we choose not to listen.—**From *Sarita's Pen*.**

BE BOLD. BUT HUMBLE

In today's society, many perceive the act of humility as a sign of being weak. For this reason, many people find it difficult to humble themselves. I have found in my short years here on earth that being humble has produced better results than being overly assertive. Humility is not humiliation. But not all can say or feel this especially if they do not know who they are in Christ. If you are confident in who you are in Christ, you will not sweat the small stuff. You can also be bold at the same time. You may ask how can this be. The key is balance. Balance is something many of us today do not have in our lives. We either have the blow with the wind mentality or the extreme structured life. There is no balance on the measuring scale. This is not easy and it takes much practice with prayer, worship and praise. This means action is required. You must do something. Dr. Martin L. King, Jr. stated it best. "I man who will not stand for something will fall or anything". Boldness requires confidence, and so does the practice of humility.—***From Sarita's Pen.***

HAPPINESS IS A CHOICE

When all else fails and it seems that you are at your end, it is then that you must reach deep down within yourself and think yourself happy. Never depend on anyone else for your happiness. True happiness is found within and it is there that the Holy Spirit is found. Job 32:8 (NLT) states "But there is a spirit within people, the breath of the Almighty within them, that makes them intelligent" Happiness is a choice.—***From Sarita's Pen***.

DO MORE THAN PRAY

There is more to praying than just the act itself. You must pray, stand still, listen, and God will give you what you need. However, whatever he gives you; it is up to you to act on it. God will not step out of glory and do for you what he gave you the power to do for yourself.—***From Sarita's Pen***

JUDGING SITUATIONS

Many times in life, we judge others situations according to our beliefs of why things may have happen or not happen to that person. If a bad thing happened to someone, some say they must have done something wrong or not pleasing to God. This is not always true. Just look at Job in the Bible. He was an upright man (Job 1:1). It rains on the just as well as the unjust. In everything that happens, God has a plan just for that situation. God ways

Prayers Flowing From Sarita's Heart & Pen

Change

Dear God, I just want to thank You for helping me make it through another day. Thank You for guiding my way, for keeping me safe, and for blessing me. Lord, please give me strength for this day. Help me to walk in the paths of righteousness for Your name's sake. I lift up my friends who are suffering with cancer and illness and for those who are grieving the loss of a loved one. Reach into their lives and provide a peace and comfort that only You can give. Fill that hurt and pain they feel with Your presence. Be their help in their times of trouble. And God, as many may be going through a great deal, let them know that there is purpose for the hurt and pain. You, God are preparing us for this season. We all must suffer, buy there is always the good news that is ever present. We all have seen and will see and experience the *But God* moments, and I thank You for them. You have never failed me and You always make everything well. It may not have been what I want all the time, but it is what I needed. For Your words tells us in Philippians 4:19 You will supply all our needs according to Your riches in glory. Glory, blessings, and honor belong to You God as I humbly submit to You and Your will as You prepare me for this season in my life. Amen!!! **Flowing From Sarita's Pen**

The Power Given to Me

Father, I thank You for another day. I am excited about the 'new'. The new life, the new blessings, and the new miracles that are on the way for Your chosen people. God today I pray that You will increase me and take me higher in my writings to be even a greater blessing to Your Kingdom. It is not about me, but it is about sharing what You have given me. God, I pray and proclaim that my ears will be opened and I hear You with greater clarity. For we all are equipped in some way to be a blessing to others as we walk in the gifts You have given us. God, I submit to You, and I pray You will manifest Yourself in every area of my life. God make me a better person, a better mother, a better sister, a better friend, a better employee, and a better preacher. God today I grasp Psalm 51:10 in which says create in me a clean heart and renew in me a right spirit. God grant favor as You have never done before for Your people so that supernatural blessings will be produced for Your Kingdom. God, as we fast and pray, I know that great and miraculous things will happen. But I am also aware of the weapons that the enemy will try to form because he knows the power of fasting and praying. God right now by the power You have given to me, I strike down every weapon that is formed. For war has been declared on Satan and his Kingdom through fasting and praying. The battle is already won for those who truly believe and proclaim. Peace, Power, Protection and Prosperity belong to us!!! Amen, Amen, and Amen!!! ***Flowing From Sarita's Pen***

Father God, I thank You for life today. I thank You for waking me up with a positive mindset. Lord I thank You today for giving me the spirit of boldness and not of fear. I thank You LORD for Your word and knowing that it is true. Lord I thank You for a reality check sometimes. For pushing me and shifting me into the position of where You want me to be and not where I want to be. You said if I just trust you, You will take care of every situation that I may be dealing with. Lord, I thank You for covering and protecting me. Thank You for the unknown instructions that don't make sense to me, but in the end they are to be followed so that You get the glory. Lord, bless Your children with peace, power, protection and prosperity. I lift those up who may be unemployed at this time. Lord, let them hear Your voice as You order their steps on their next job assignment. In Hebrews 13:5, You state that You would never leave or forsake Your people. Lord, guide our footsteps and our tongues so when we speak, we speak under Your influence and not our own. For Your people in the workplace, give us a fresh anointing to do our jobs today as we strive to transform and set the tone. Lord, forgive us of our sins as we forgive those who sinned against us. Let us not have a self-righteous attitude and walk as a hypocrite. For all have sinned and fallen short of Your glory. God let us all have a forgiving, determined and fighting spirit knowing that the rewards will be great. God today, I proclaim, declare and decree that the "It" You placed in my life will manifest to bring about a blessed life not only for me but for ALL Your children who are obedient and unselfish. God as we go on this journey to pursue the "It" You have given us, I asked You to cover and protect us from Satan's deceptions that will come strong. But God, we are not worried for we know who has our back. It is so!!! Amen!!!

Flowing From Sarita's Heart & Pen

God, I thank You for today. Thank You for a song in my heart this morning that says" hold on be strong: it will be alright". God, I thank You for the spirit of perseverance. Thank You for the big HGIC (Holy Ghost In Charge). I feel Your presence and I embrace it. I know that today is a day that will be like no other. This is a day that You have made, and a day that the right decisions will be made. God, deliver and clear my paths of foolish people. But God, if I have to encounter them, give me a word for them. There is work to do and I don't have time to deal with the foolishness. But Lord most of all, let me exam myself to make sure I am not the foolish one. You, God are the source of my strength. What You give me, the world can't take it away. God, I rebuke and bind the spirit of defeat. It has no room in the lives of Your people. In Your word, You state that I am more than conquer. I speak this in the air today. I decree and declare victory today for someone today. I don't know who it is, but they have overcome and many will follow this same pattern. O my God, today is the first day of many days of victory and the devil in hell can't stop it. The many manifestations that are about to take place are once more proof that I win. The war has already been won. God, I am what You say I am and I can have what You say I can have. God as Your child, everything I touch shall turn to gold. Your word that goes out shall not return void. I pray for those no one else is praying for. Bless everyone praying this prayer. I pray for a supernatural transformation. God, You are The Great I Am; The all-powerful God. I give You all the glory and all the praise for You are more than worthy to be praised. We have the victory. It is so! Amen. **From Sarita's Heart & Pen**

God, I thank You this morning for placing virtuous women in my life. You always know what or who is best for me. God thank You for another day's journey as I apply what I have learned from these virtuous women You have placed in my life. Lord these women have given me advice, and their lives are examples of virtuous women. I am firm believer that You can learn from anyone. I speak blessings into the lives of woman who have blessed me and are not aware of it. The blessings may not always have been viewed by man as big, but they were life changing for me. God, I speak blessings over our little girls today. They are growing up in a time where woman are overly aggressive. God, I speak balance in the air over this situation. God we as women have a great deal on our plates sometimes, but God You made us so they we can handle difficult situations. God, I thank You for the power of prayer to cry out to You when the load gets heavy. You are a miracle worker, and You have never failed me. Thank You God for Your mercy and grace I see daily. God please bless each woman who maybe going through trials and tribulations right now. As she calls upon You, give her peace and let her know that You have her back. God in You there are 'no limits' in goodness, mercy and blessings. I thank You in advance for their breakthrough. It is so! Amen. **From Sarita's Heart & Pen**

GOD'S GREATNESS

God, You are the source of my strength and You are my song. You are my guide, and You are the only 'one'. Thank You for supplying all my needs and giving me what I need daily in the spirit and the physical. God, I thank You for giving me what I need and not always what I want. You know what is best for me. Guide my footsteps and guide my tongue to speak Your words and not my own. God, I ask You to bless today, and supply all needs in life. I pray that each of our faith will be made stronger in You and trust You in every area of life. God You are the one true source to supply each of us with what is needed. Where there is confusion, give clarity. Where there is hurt, give comfort. Where there is frustration, give peace in the situation. God let each know today that there is nothing that will happen that You cannot handle. Amen! ***Flowing From Sarita's Heart & Pen***

Great is Your faithfulness God. Every morning, I see evidence of Your glory, mercy and power. I thank You for being faithful even when man is not; even when I am not faithful to You or myself. You are 'Jehovah God'. I thank You for giving me a word to speak to Your people and the people even when it is not always received. I will continue to believe You even when there is chaos all around. I believe and proclaim that You will breathe life into every dying situation. I believe and proclaim that You will heal bodies of cancer and restore the broken heart. I believe and proclaim that You will restore finances. I believe and proclaim that You will restore relationships. I believe and proclaim that our children are victorious and have bright futures. I believe and proclaim that You will be invited back into the school system and order will be restored. I believe and proclaim that this country will return to "In God We Trust". The time is now that we must stand for something or we will fall for anything. God sometimes I grow tired, but Your word Galatians 6:9 (NLT) keeps me going; "And let us not be weary in well doing: for in due season we shall reap, if we faint not". Thank You for Your word that empowers and activates my faith. I believe You for greater peace, greater power, greater protection and greater prosperity. Not just for me, but for all of Your sons and daughters. I decree! Amen.—***From Sarita's Heart and Pen***

God, I thank You for Your faithfulness. I am reminded daily as I see new mercies of just how faithful You are. As I go through situations, I look back over past situations in my life that You brought me through, and I receive peace. I know that You will make a way as I stay faithful to You. Lord, I am ever so grateful for this life You have given me. You provide and protect me daily. God bless me from the crown of my head to the soles of my feet. God give me a fresh supply of strength to do my job. Anoint every project and every idea so that even the smallest accomplishment will bring YOU glory. God remind me of Your grace and mercy that brought me through. God, I pray for an attitude of gratitude for there is none like You Jehovah God who is the eternal self-existing one who keeps his covenant promises to his covenant people. God, I don't ever want to forget what You brought me through as I take these test as testimonies to others of Your greatness. God sometimes Satan will try to bring back the bad memories from the past. He has no place nor power in the past, present or future. For when he tries to remind You of Your past . . . . You remind him of his future. For as Your children God, we are pressing forward only looking back to remember Your goodness. AMEN—*From Sarita's Heart & Pen.*

God, I thank You for being excellent in all Your ways. You made me in Your image and I should always strive to be like You LORD. I thank You God for the Holy Spirit that works in me and gives me the power to overcome. Thank You for loving me and keeping me in Your care. Thank You for protection. God, I pray for those no one is praying for. Everything that You make is good. I speak encouragement into the atmosphere. God I am a Kings Kid, I do not accept anything less than the best. 1 John 4:4 (NLT) states "But You belong to God, my dear children. You have already won a victory over those people, because the Spirit who lives in You is greater than the spirit who lives in the world." God I am standing on Your promises and not mans. Man will let You down. Thank You for new mercies I see daily. God I see a prosperous future. The past is the past and has no power over our future. All these things, I proclaim, declare and decree. It is so! Amen *From Sarita's Heart & Pen.*

SELF-AWARENESS

Good morning God. I want to thank You for another day that was not promised. God today I come against a judgmental spirit and unconstructive criticism. God You tell us continuously throughout the Bible not to judge others. Luke 6:37(NLT) tell us to not judge others, and we will not be judged. Do not condemn others, or it will all come back against us. Forgive others, and we will be forgiven. I am glad to know that You have the last say so. You are the final judge of man. Many times we develop this self-righteous attitude that causes us to judge others, but what we fail to remember is that it was You God who showed us mercy and grace when we messed up. God, I stop and thank You right now for this!!!. Move today and convict us in our spirits when we want to judge others. God You are a loving and forgiving God. You are a God of second chances. Amen!!! **Flowing From Sarita's Heart & Pen.**

Good morning God and thank You for another day that was not promised to me. God today I speak life into every dead situation. God, I pray for those no one else is praying for. Today God, I speak positive energy into the atmosphere. God, I speak against all negative and judgmental speaking that we as Christians can put forth out of ignorance and stupidity sometimes. God, I pray that we learn to develop the *spirit of shut up*. For You state in Proverbs 13:3 (NTL) that those who control their tongue will have a long life, that opening our mouths can ruin everything. God, You also tell us in Proverbs 15:2 (NLT) that the tongue of the wise makes knowledge appealing, but the mouth of a fool belches out foolishness. And last in Proverbs 15:4 (NLT) You state that gentle words are a tree of life, but a deceitful tongue crushes the spirit. God let us not be accused of assassination of others spirits. For no one should want blood on their hands and be called a murderer. God, I speak death to every demon on assignment who put their mouth on Your people. God, I stand on Your word and keep it my heart. I pronounce, proclaim, and decree that everything prayed will come to pass. We will be more

conscious of our words. It is so!!! Amen. ***Flowing "Strongly"
From Sarita's Heart & Pen.***

God thank You for Your word that tells us to not be weary in well
doing, and if we hold on, we will receive many blessings. Today
God, I thank You for Your mercy and grace. Thank You for not
giving me what I deserve. Forgive me for my sins as I forgive
those who have sinned against me. God in all that I do, I seek
to acknowledge You. Bless those no one else is praying for and
convict us in our spirit when we develop a self-righteous attitude.
For all have done wrong in Your sight. God many times people
are in situations, and they are not aware of how to handle them.
God, I pray that they would seek You in every area of their lives
not depending on themselves. Sometime act as our own god.
God You are the only wise and living God that will supply all our
needs and deliver us even from situations that we put ourselves
in. God let us talk less and learn how to development a 'shut up'
and a non-judgmental spirit. God we should take action more
to pray more for our sisters and brothers instead of putting our
mouth on them in a negative way. God bless today. Speak to us
and direct our steps so that we are pleasing to You. God, I speak
against every weapon that is being formed against Your people.
For it will not succeed. Amen!!! ***Flowing From Sarita's Pen***

God all blessings and honor belong to You today. God, I thank
You and bless You for the relationship that I have with You. For
You are always there and keep me on the right path even when
I try to take a detour sometimes. The path always leads back to
You. LORD I thank You for Your miracles and blessings. Thank
You for equipping me to handle situations in my life. I always
say God there is nothing that will happen today that YOU and I
can't handle. God, I pray for everyone praying this prayer with
me. I pray that You increase their faith, humble their spirits and
give them Your peace. Let us be receptive of Your word and not
quick to anger or falsely accuse due to our own insecurities. We
are human, but we are accountable once we know Your truth.
Luke 12:48 (NLT) states "But someone who does not know,
and then does something wrong, will be punished only lightly.

When someone has been given much, much will be required in return; and when someone has been entrusted with much, even more will be required." God, I pray for unusual miracles today, but I also pray that You equipped each to handle what will come before the miracle. You are an awesome God and serving You is not hard, but we must submit to You and Your will to fully receive Your blessings. Many times, we must stop worshiping other people, ourselves, and those little gods in order to do that. Bless today and the miracles You will perform. Amen!!! **Flowing From Sarita's Pen**

God, I am ever so grateful for just being and belonging to You. God, You know sometimes things happen to us in life that produces a spirit of shut down. We are tempted to not be the giving and loving person we are called to be and it is hard to get back on track. But God, I thank You for the people that You place in my life. I thank You for the Holy Spirit that speaks to me, comforts me and lets me know that all is well and to be patient. I so strongly grasp Galatians 6:9 (NLT); "And let us not be weary in well doing: for in due season we shall reap, if we faint not". God please minister to everyone praying this prayer with me. I pray their day is productive in You and that each will help someone today and live not just for themselves. God please forgive us for our spirit of selfishness. In Luke 9:23, Jesus tells us that if we want to follow him, we must turn from our selfish ways, and take up our cross daily, and follow him. The rewards are great. Greater peace, power, protection and prosperity is ours. The world teaches us to be selfish in every area of our lives from the advertising on TV to some of the music we listen to. This is the trick of the enemy. Selfishness will lead to unhappy lives, loneliness and yes even destruction. God, I rebuke the spirit of selfishness and all the devastation that comes with it. God we can be our own worst enemy by living only for ourselves. I also pray each of us live a life that is pleasing to You. God there is nothing like Your peace. God, I pray that this prayer is received by Your people and that their thought process will change and they will be a blessing today and in the future. It is so!!! Amen!!! *Flowing from Sarita's Heart & Pen.*

LOVE & RELATIONSHIPS

God today I thank You for the relationships that are productive and even for the ones that are not for they help to make me a stronger person. But the most important relationship I thank You for is the relationship with You LORD. I thank You for taking care of me and speaking to me and always being faithful even as I and some others maybe going through a period of re-thinking, re-establishing, and reconciliation. God I focus and meditate on my relationship with You, I pray for others You have placed in my life. There is a time and season for everything. God speak to me and let me to hear with Your ears the directions I need to take. I pray for clarity and when You speak to me. Lord, I pray as Saint Francis of Assisi prayed "Lord grant me the Serenity to accept the things I cannot change, Courage to change the things I can, and the Wisdom to know the difference." I speak greater blessings. Build up my sisters and brothers. I pray they reach down and help another sister or brother. Amen. *From Sarita's Heart & Pen.*

PROTECTION

My Heavenly Father, I thank You for Your wisdom and guidance each day. It is so exciting to walk in Your ways. I appreciate the unexpected blessings You bring my way each day. Thank You for the wonderful people You have placed in my life. Lord, give me the discernment to recognize those things that are not of You. Give me spiritual eyesight to see things that are of the enemy so that I might not be fooled by him. Keep me from anger and help me to know Your will so that I can follow You closely in all of my ways. Bless my family, friends, and keep them from the Satan's traps. I ask this in the name of Jesus Christ. Amen!!! *Flowing From Sarita's Pen*

STRENGTH

God today I thank You for freedom in the spirit. Thank You for living in a country where I am free to praise and worship You as I please. God many times we take this freedom for granted. God, I ask You to guide my footsteps and guide my tongue. God, I strive to consult You in making decisions in every area of our lives from relationships, finances, and yes careers. God, I thank You for blessing me in every area of my life. God thank You for being free in You. To trust You with everything that I am and I have. I am nothing without You in my life. God, I pray for those that are struggling with major decisions right now. I pray each will give all their concerns to You and leave them with You. I don't care how many degrees I have and who I know, I can't be truly successful without You in my life. God, I pray for continued humility and patience. For I know and have experience that You always work things out for my good. God, I pray that all will grow to be and live free in You not caring what the world may think. God, I pray that we will push forward and liberate ourselves of all the distractions believing that we can do all things through You. God place the right people in our lives to help us be the people in You that we need to be. It is so!!!! Amen!!! **Flowing From Sarita's Pen.**

God, I thank You today for watching over Your children and warning us when danger is ahead. God forgive us of our transgressions as we forgive those who have wronged us with an action or even unpleasant words. In 1 John 4:20 (NLT) You tell us if someone says, "I love God," but hates a Christian brother or sister, that person is a liar; for if we don't love people we can see, how can we love God, whom we cannot see? God, I thank You for Your omnipresence. Today God, I thank You for a newer outlook on life and even a brighter future as You have moved in a mighty way by restoring my mind with even more positive energy. I know and feel that Your servants are about to receive great blessings. I know from experience that some blessings may not come as we may think, but all work out for our good. God, I pray that each will devote their lives to You in every area of their lives.

God, I pray for a deeper discernment and understanding. For the enemy is seeking to destroy what You God have blessed. God, I pray that Your servants will be very watchful for the wolves in sheep clothing that seem harmless but can hinder progress and even destroy. God bless our children and protect them today also from those little demons that seem harmless. For the delicate and innocent minds are the main targets of the enemy. But I pray with power and rebuke all liars and every form of untruth that is spoken against Your people. For whatever untruths that are told will be as a boomerang. It will come back with a greater force. Bless today God as You manifest. God, I Am On Top!!! And I believe every word You have spoken into my life and the lives of each one of my sisters and brother. Amen!!! ***Flowing From Sarita's Heart & Pen***

God there is an old spiritual song that has a verse that states "If You can't help me, please don't stop me. Move out of my way, don't try to block me." God, I pray for this day the *spirit of helps*. Let us help our sisters and brothers who are in need. Even though some may say I don't have anything to give, but God there is always a way to help even in the middle of our own situations. We must think beyond ourselves. God, I pray that each person reading this message will reach out to someone. God, I thank You for Your guidance that has taught me how to forget about my situations and be a blessing to others. Many times when I give You my issues and concentrate on helping others, You resolve my situation before I even notice it. God are awesome in all that You do, and with You there is no failure. I bless You and thank You for every opportunity to be a blessing to others. Amen!!! ***Flowing From Sarita's Pen***

ADVERSITY/DISTRACTIONS

God today I thank You for another day of life and a second chance. God thank You for listening to me and letting me know that everything that comes up in my life is not an emergency. God right now I pray for those who may be suffering from anxiety attacks and not be aware of their condition. I speak healing right now. God, I pray for strength and boldness today for those who maybe letting their issue(s) get the best of them. We all must learn how to push through our issues and depend on You and not ourselves. God You are awesome and there is none like You even though we try to make people and things our god(s). There is only one true living God, and that is You Jehovah God (The eternal self-existing one who keeps his covenant promises to his covenant people). We will keep standing, praying, and moving forward leaving those things behind that are not of You. For these things will only lead to failure. But we serve a mighty God!!! Victory is our name. Amen!!! **Flowing From Sarita's Heart & Pen**

God, I thank You so much for Your guidance and direction. God, I thank You for blessing me with the spirit of discernment. God in all Your ways I acknowledge that You are awesome and all powerful. God today I come praying and covering Your people. I pray that each will move even closer to You today. God, I pray that each will walk in Your ways because the enemy is looking for anything to discredit and destroy Your people. We cannot and will not give him that satisfaction. God, I especially pray for our Youth. Cover them and keep them in Your care. God we as Christians must stay focus because there are some many intentional distractions to throw us off course. But God, I pray that each will stand on Your word. 1 Corinthians 15:58(NLT) tells us to be strong and immovable. Always work enthusiastically for the Lord, for nothing that we do for the Lord is ever useless. I declare and decree that we will withstand the attacks that we face. God has and will equip us to deal with any situation. There is nothing today that will happen that God and I can't handle. Focus shall we be. It is so!!!! Amen! **Flowing From Heart & Sarita's Pen.**

Worshiping You God in spirit and in truth is what I seek. Thank You for another day and another week. It has been a little challenging God, but I am still here and full of joy. God, I thank You for new mercies I see daily. Thank You for blessings and favor. God today I come praying for my sisters and brothers that they yield not to the temptations that Satan tries to set before them. God let them adhere to Your word and do what is right and pleasing to You. God Bless each person today reading this message. I speak that they hear You with clarity. This is not a season of recession but a season of reap-cession (harvest) for the Saints. God we give You glory and know that You always work things out for our good. I thank You God for Your faithfulness. Amen!!! *Flowing from Sarita's Pen.*

God forgive me of my sins as I forgive those who have sinned against me. Lord today I pray for the breaking of strongholds once again as this is a major issue with many Christians. God today I pray that all will begin to deal with these issues in order to be free and live life well in Christ. God, I pray that each will confess their sins. In the name of Jesus, I pronounce, proclaim and decree that each will speak life into their lives by breaking any generational curses that may have been spoken many years ago. God for we have a covenant with You and through the blood of Jesus Christ. We are joined to You LORD, and are one spirit with You. God we divorce ourselves from any evil spirits or demons on assignment that would cause chaos in our lives. Let Your glory be our covering and protect our homes, children, family, and finances. The power of darkness will submit to Your power God. There is a better life. Amen!!! **Flowing From Sarita's Pen**

Good morning God and thank You for Your brand new mercies I see today. For You are worthy to be praised by happy voices for all Your excellence. God today I pray that each will look for the blessings in every situation. The blessing may not always be for them, but for someone else. God some of our biggest obstacles in life is the lack of wanting to see the blessing of others, and not reproving selfishness. God create in those a clean heart and renew in them the right spirit. It is not always about us. We must move past this behavior and celebrate with those who have been blessed. God, I speak peace into the lives of those who are facing adversity right now. God open their eyes to see what

You are really trying to do in their lives when adversity arises. God strengthen them and give them joy in the middle of their circumstance. God if we truly seek You, You will provide us with answers we are looking for. I pray that each will humble themselves and hear You when You speak. I pray for the removal of all distractions. I pray that each will focus on the good things that You have provided and know that if You did it once, You will do it again. For the spirit can be blessed just by knowing and believing this. Amen!!! ***Flowing From Sarita's Pen***

ENCOURAGEMENT

God, I thank You for another day of being *blessed to be a blessing.* Thank You for the people who speak life into me and encourage me daily. God as this happens; it empowers me more to be a blessing through the gifts You have given me especially the gift of writing. Thank You for the insight and being able to encourage Your people. It is not always easy and sometimes I don't feel like being kind to ungrateful and unkind people, but God here I stand, striving daily to maintain a humble spirit and a giving heart. For I know it is You that works in me. I can only be who You design me to be. Lord, today I come boldly praying for my sisters and brother that they develop the spirit of helps. Giving back to others what You have blessed them with. God, I pray that each of us not be selfish with the blessings, gifts, and talents that You have given each and every one of us. These gifts are not just for our own selfish needs. You gave us these gifts to build up Your Kingdom, and tear down the strongholds of Satan. God, I come to say thank You!!!!! I say thank You and bless You for all who are too arrogant, prideful or nasty to say *Thank You LORD.* God we must realize that we are placed on this earth for You. You will supply all our needs. It is You who shows favor to those who are obedient to You. It is You who closes and opens doors that lead to promotions . . . . not man. It is You God who love us and love us well. It is You God that is the true center of our joy. God, I feel and see doors opening, lives changing, and an overflow of blessings on Your people. These are those who have been patiently waiting. Our time is now! Amen. **Flowing From Sarita's Heart & Pen**

PEACE

God today I come thanking You for just being God. Thank You for looking out for me; blessing me and making me a blessing for someone else. Thank You for peace and placing me in situations where I am learning to have greater patience, because with patience comes maturity. Thank You for both. Thank You for the trials and tribulations that I have gone through. They continue to make me stronger; stronger to handle, deal with and help others on a higher level. God we are placed on this earth to service You and to be a blessing to others. Bless all who pray this prayer to be a blessing and not be selfish with what You have blessed them with. We are a blessed country and a people. God, I pray for those no one else is praying for. I pray for our sisters and brothers in Haiti that are suffering. LORD, I speak super national blessings for them. Send Your angels to provide for and protect the ones who are still alive but have not been found. God bless and give peace to the families in the US who have lost family members in Haiti or who are not sure if family members are still alive. God it is this time that our spiritual maturity level is tested. God, in You I put my trust, and I know that all things will work together for Your good. I rebuke the spirit of selfishness and greed that normally take place in times like these. The enemy has no room if we as Your children would not stand for it and do the right things. God, I thank You for making a way out of no way. For You LORD are the author and finisher of my fate. It is so! Amen. **From Sarita's Heart & Pen.**